Community-Based Instruction: A Guidebook for Teachers

Barbara A. Beakley
Sandy L. Yoder
Lynda L. West

Council for
Exceptional
Children

Library of Congress Cataloging-in-Publication Data

Beakley. Barbara A., 1950-
    Community-based instruction: a guidebook for teachers/Barbara Beakley, Sandy L. Yoder, Lynda L. West.
        p. cm.
    Includes bibliographical references.
    ISBN 0-86586-983-9
    1. Community education—United States. 2. People with disabilities—Education—United States. 3. Life skills—Study and teaching—United States. I. Yoder, Sandy L, 1962- II. West, Lynda L. III. Title.

    LC1036.5.B43 2003
    371.19—dc21

                                                    2003055366

ISBN 0-86586-983-9

Copyright 2003 by Council for Exceptional Children, 1110 North Glebe Road, Suite 300, Arlington, Virginia 22201-5704

Stock No. P5630

Printed in the United States of America

10 9 8 7 6 5 4 3 2 1

Table of Contents

Acknowledgements

The preparation of this book was based upon years of work with children and young adults learning practical, independent skills within their classroom, school and community. We acknowledge that without the many lessons they taught us, we would not be able to share these methods with you.

A group of professional individuals shared their expertise and valuable technical support. We would like to thank Susan King, Mickey Wircenski, Arden Boyer-Stephens, Edward Heisig, Sally Bredeman, and Wes Yoder for their suggestions, many readings and willingness to help us complete this project.

We have been greatly supported by our families and employers throughout the many drafts and challenges of working and writing. However, none have provided more help, patience and encouragement than Tim Yoder and Ed Beakley.

Preface

Community-based instruction is a method that was utilized long before the formal mandates of special education and, in some form, will continue through the many reforms, reauthorizations and methodology research that are on the horizon. Everyone in education is experiencing the dynamics of teaching learning in this fast-paced, highly technical world where accessibility, standards and accountability are shaping the general curriculum for all students. With the knowledge that local philosophy and operating resources vary greatly, there is always a need for good instruction. Quality instruction and the methods used to support student learning are based on the needs of the students, not a particular place. If the needs of your students and the initiatives of your school call for instruction in the community, enclosed are some resources, ideas, and procedures to help you implement a systematic approach to augment your instructional strategies.

As this book goes to press, the reauthorization of IDEA is imminent. In trusting that the basics of education for individual with disabilities will remain at the core of the new mandate, it is conceivable that there will be new recommendations for ensuring that all students receive the education they deserve. In the years since the 1997 reauthorization, states have worked to implement a federal program titled, No Child Left Behind. We have seen the impetus of this program striving to enhance the learning of all students and to measure the growth in learning throughout their educational experience. This serves as another indicator that the quality of instruction is foremost in the minds of states, educators and families.

It is hoped that this book gives you a collection of ideas that can be adapted to your school's program and applicable to your community. Teacher-made assessment tools are included to evaluate if the method of instruction, in this case community-based instruction, is effective and students are gaining independent skills. We encourage you to look at this process as one that allows you determine the needs of your students and adjust the suggestions included to make your instruction of the best quality possible, instruction that promotes measurable gains in the students you serve.

Barbara A. Beakley

Chapter 1

An Orientation to Community-Based Instruction

What Is Community-Based Instruction (CBI)?

Community-Based Instruction is a strategy used to promote functional skills in natural, nonschool environments that students frequent individually, with their families, or with peers. All students can benefit from receiving instruction in natural environments. In some cases instruction may occur in a work setting, in others, a recreation or leisure setting. When considering the total curriculum for individuals with disabilities, the goals, content, and location of instruction are important factors in educational planning. Community-Based Instruction (CBI) is the portion of instruction that occurs in the community after classroom instruction has taken place. CBI is intended to ensure that students achieve functional skills in the environments where those skills will be used naturally.

Why Is CBI Important?

Jennifer Jones is 19. She needs extensive support on a daily basis in her educational programming and independent living skills. Jennifer wants to live in an apartment, go to work, and buy her own clothes. Her teachers have just a few years to work with Jennifer and her family to accomplish those goals. Jennifer's independence will not occur if she spends the next two years in a totally traditional academic classroom. Success depends on Jennifer receiving instruction in natural environments in the community where she lives.

The results of using CBI as an instructional strategy are far-reaching. When parents see their young adult family member who has a disability independently enter the community, there is no question that the skills learned using CBI are important. Adult service agencies notice that students who receive instruction in the community are much better prepared to work in competitive and supported employment and live in supervised or semi-independent living arrangements. In addition to personal factors, there are legislative and quality programming issues that support the use of CBI as an instructional method for students with disabilities. Among the most relevant are the following:

- CBI recognizes comprehensive school reform issues.
- CBI adheres to legislative mandates for individuals with disabilities (e.g., ADA, IDEA).
- CBI supports transition planning.
- CBI complies with the achievement of standards.
- CBI relates to the New American High School movement.
- CBI utilizes performance-based assessment.
- CBI reflects systematic, ecological instruction.
- CBI promotes the transfer of skills from the classroom to the community.
- CBI is developmentally appropriate and age-appropriate.
- CBI fosters problem-solving.
- CBI ensures continuity across the life-skills curriculum.
- CBI creates acceptance in the community and local partnerships.

The following explanation takes each of the areas listed above and expands upon the importance of CBI in relation to those specific areas.

Comprehensive School Reform

Comprehensive school reform represents a set of issues and concerns that address school-wide improvement, which includes vision, planning, and well-informed faculty who initiate curricular change on behalf of all students. The concept represents global changes in all aspects of the educational process—from management to instruction. The goals of comprehensive school reform are to prepare students for the ever-changing society they will enter. It is hoped that global changes for all students in all aspects of the educational process will include curricular changes for students with support needs. As schools make changes in delivery, location, and methodology for all students, this could increase the need for more use of CBI.

Legislative Mandates

The most influential legislation for all students with support needs was The Education for All Handicapped Children Act of 1975, P.L. 94-142. That legislation paved the way for many of the practices that currently direct special education, such as the Individualized Education Program (IEP), free appropriate public education, least restrictive environment, due process, and several other factors that ensure quality education for students identified as requiring special education. Students with support needs in secondary grades were greatly affected by the original legislation because it guaranteed their education, and it afforded them education until they reached age 21. In many cases this extended the students' time in school and allowed them to benefit from the increased instructional time and social and academic opportunities.

The Individuals with Disabilities Education Act (IDEA) of 1990, P.L. 101-476, was a very influential amendment to P.L. 94-142 for secondary students. Among many additions and clarifications to the original law and later amendments, IDEA specifically outlined transition services. According to Sitlington, Clark, and Kolstoe (2000), transition services must begin by age 16, be initiated by special educators, involve the students, and include personnel from adult service agencies. According to the Department of Education (1992), transition services were defined as:

> A coordinated set of activities for a student, designed within an outcome-oriented process, that promotes movement from school to postschool activities, including postsecondary education, vocational training, integrated employment (including supported employment), continuing and adult education, adult services, independent living, or community participation. (p. 44804)

This legislation gave teachers strong incentives to plan for students with support needs who were entering the last phase of their public education and to connect students with adult services.

Although the reauthorization of IDEA in 1997, P.L. 105-17, maintained that transition as an outcomes-based process consists of a coordinated set of activities bridging the gap between high school and the adult world, the newer law used more explicit language and age guidelines. First, beginning at age 14, the Individualized Transition Plan (ITP) focuses on the student's courses of study and becomes a component of the IEP. Second, by age 16, the IEP team must make a statement of transition services, including interagency responsibilities and needed linkages. Finally, at least 1 year before the student reaches the age of majority, the age that is considered adulthood in each state, the student should be informed of the rights that will transfer to them upon reaching that age (Turnbull & Cilley, 1999).

Over the span of several years, a series of mandates have affected the content of and participation in vocational, career, and technology training. These include the Carl D. Perkins Vocational Education Act of 1984, the Carl D. Perkins Vocational and Applied Technology Education Act Amendments of 1990, and the Carl D. Perkins Vocational and Applied Technology Educational Act Amendments of 1998. The act and amendments greatly impact on the focus of vocational education, who participates in it, and how it can create meaningful outcomes. Initially, the Perkins legislation emphasized that *all* students should be exposed to all of the available options for career paths prior to choosing high school courses. This included students who planned to enter academic and vocational fields, as well as students with disabilities. This legislation emphasized increasing academic subject matter and technology in vocational education programs. Additional legislation such as the School-to-Work Opportunities Act of 1994 and Workforce Investment Act of 1998 emphasized community partnerships, the interaction of schools and businesses, and the involvement of school programs in helping students find work opportunities following the secondary school program.

Transition Planning

Following the important legislative mandates listed earlier, especially IDEA 1990, schools began to examine secondary programs for students with disabilities. The period of planning for transition begins when students reach age 14 and can choose their courses of study. When students reach age 16, their postsecondary outcomes become part of the IEP. At 21, students reach the end of mandated public schooling. Students who maintain pace with their classes and complete IEP goals may graduate a few years before they reach 21 and continue to the next phase of their plans. These years were designated to evaluate student interests, abilities, and preferences; set goals in transition areas; and provide students with the educational experiences necessary to meet those goals. Transition planning is a systematic process that looks at the areas of postsecondary training, employment, independent living, and community participation. While the emphasis here is community participation, the areas are interrelated. Transition planning is a comprehensive and dynamic process that concentrates on the areas needing specialized instruction within, or apart from, the general curriculum. This overview will highlight setting goals, writing plans, and implementing those plans in school and in the community.

Typically by high school, students have some idea of areas they find interesting and those in which they excel. Family encouragement, the influence of significant others, and many outside forces affect what high school students envision for themselves and their futures. For some students with varied levels of support needs, these planning efforts have not been as deliberate as required by the law. One process that supports the establishment of goals and individual planning for the future is known as person-centered planning. This concept outlines ways that families, service providers, and individuals can look at and plan for the future. Wehman (1998) emphasized this process by saying:

> All person-centered planning approaches begin with the belief that all individuals, regardless of the type or severity of their disabilities, not only benefit from services provided by their communities, but also offer their communities many gifts and capacities. It follows then that all people should live and be contributing members of their communities. (p. 25)

Wehman continues to describe person-centered planning in relation to the networks and community supports that are considered in planning for the future. Person-centered planning supports transition planning by helping teams define goals and state strategies to help students achieve their goals. It enhances transition planning by defining supports and actions to implement transition plans that provide continuity and show progress toward students' goals. Whether a transition planning team follows a specific planning process or a general transition planning format determined by the school district, the first item is to determine and set outcomes which lead to IEP goals.

All students who receive specialized services have an IEP as part of their educational program. Until students begin to plan their transition to adult life, IEPs are curriculum-based. At age 16, the transition plan becomes an initial part of the IEP. Students, parents, educators, and related service providers begin to write down the desired outcomes of the student. The transition plan then influences IEP goals and outside services that will take over programming when students exit the school system. According to McDonnell, Mathot-Buckner, and Ferguson (1996), "Transition planning brings together students, parents, and professionals to identify and develop the skills and resources necessary to ensure successful postschool adjustment" (p. 33).

Transition planning is an ongoing process of defining outcomes, writing plans, and implementing those plans in all settings necessary for students to achieve their desired outcomes. The level of concentration in any one area depends on students' outcomes and their support needs in reaching those outcomes. As a strategy to support student independence and problem-solving, CBI is one way to implement some portions of the transition plan. Implementation of transition planning is individual and should be accomplished within the regular curriculum as much as possible. When the situation calls for employment or implementation in the community, those locations are part of the implementation. The key to successful transition planning includes concentrated effort in all areas to help students accomplish their outcomes and make connections for support in adult life.

Standards

States set educational standards in an attempt to serve young citizens and meet federal mandates. McDonnell, McLaughlin, and Morison (1997), in their report, *Educating One and All*, highlighted the challenges that special education teachers face trying to intersect special education policy with standards-based reform. McDonnell et al. (1997) emphasized that the goals of standards-based reform—such as raising expectations, improving outcomes, and strengthening curriculum—are valuable issues in special education as well as in general education. The goal of standards-based reform, McDonnell et al. (1997) believe, is to increase accountability in a uniform way for all students, including students who require special education.

Educators are concerned about implementing standards for diverse learners. Kluth and Straut (2001) point out that there are several kinds of diversity in today's classroom. We see increased diversity of students' religious backgrounds, students with disabilities spending part of their day in the general classroom, students with a primary language other than English, much broader cultural diversity, and a highly mobile student population. As standards affect curriculum, instruction, and assessment, participation of all students creates a comprehensive school program for everyone. In order for this to occur, standards must be flexible—allowing for various stages of development—and include a wide range of assessment methods. Every student should participate in meaningful and stimulating educational programs and all stakeholders in the school and community should contribute to the process. In the process, use of adaptations helps make the curriculum relevant and authentic assessment occurs during instruction. Therefore, if the curriculum is affected by standards for all students and everyone has access to improvements, all students benefit from the standards-based change.

The concept of constructing knowledge from various sources of information occurs consistently in standards-based reform. Community-Based Instruction works on the premise that students can build upon experiences gathered from various locations within the community. CBI also focuses on how students acquire skills. The practice of teaching students in the community depends on the student's ability to perform acquired skills. Standards-based reform and CBI are compatible in so far as they both express reasonable criteria that all students are to achieve.

New American High School

The New American High School initiative focuses on challenging academic standards and using new instructional techniques to prepare students for postsecondary training and careers. The concept supports students in secondary schools by improving their professional development, using community-based experiences to enhance their classroom learning, and helping them develop partnerships with community members. Community input in planning curricula is encouraged. This concept directly relates to the CBI goal of preparing students for adult life. The benefits students with disabilities achieve through such initiatives are crucial to the overall goals of school reform.

Performance-Based Assessment

When Dana, a 10th grader, and Bob, a student with moderate disabilities, go to a restaurant for lunch, Bob carries tissues, money, a calculator, a picture menu, a tax chart, and a tipping card. Bob's teacher carries a checklist of the skills he is expected to demonstrate and sits at a nearby table. Dana and Bob order their meal, eat, and pay the bill themselves. Dana expects Bob to perform every step himself and will only help Bob upon his request. As Bob and Dana are paying the bill, Bob's teacher marks the skills that he performed independently. The evaluation of Bob's performance is an ongoing process used throughout his program.

Direct observation of skills in the community remains the primary way to determine that students have mastered independent living objectives. While nearly every state has implemented formal assessment criteria of academic skills, most states have not decided how students who receive special education services fit into the state assessment process. Theoretically, authentic assessment is accepted nationwide, but in reality a truly "hands-on" assessment in the community has been slow to emerge. In the meantime, teachers continue to base performance measures upon direct and indirect observation of students' actions in natural settings.

Systematic, Ecological Instruction

Instruction is designed to help students expand existing skills into functional, independent behaviors. A systematic instructional approach enables students to progress sequentially from simple to complex issues and increases their mastery of skills. Ecological instruction requires much of the teaching and learning to occur in the actual location where the skill is used. Initially teachers determine the sequence of instruction by analyzing the student's skill and developing an instructional plan. The teacher assesses the student's performance to determine where the student has mastered skills in order to begin instruction. Finally, teachers integrate extensive repeated practice into the ongoing plan to assure that a new skill becomes part of the student's repertoire.

Both new and experienced teachers frequently are overwhelmed when trying to plan for a heterogeneous classroom. Because teachers must manage multiple planning and teaching duties, a well-planned, systematic program is more effective than a spontaneous approach. The challenge is to get the planning component of the program into a manageable process that will allow enough time for implementation, assessment, and research. To meet that challenge, teachers can create a CBI plan that will begin immediately with students learning in actual environments, which will allow for students' sequential growth in independence. The key to manageable planning is for teachers to set realistic, personal goals and design a system that eventually self-perpetuates. The plan may be location-based, in which students learn all of the skills needed in one location, or skill-based, meaning that one skill, such as pedestrian safety, is taught in many different locations. Regardless, steady pacing, good organization, and effective data collection are imperative.

Transfer of Skills

Often, the application or transfer of skills from one environment to the next occurs naturally. For example, riding a school bus is good preparation for riding a public bus in that one climbs aboard, takes a seat, and remains seated until the destination is reached. There are many differences as well. First, riders of a public bus must decide which bus will go to their desired destinations. There must be some form of payment. Finally, riders must decide when to indicate to the driver that they are ready to exit. Furthermore, how is riding a subway or local rail system similar to riding a bus? How do students apply the knowledge of destination and arrival when there is no two-way conversation with the driver? How does the teacher prepare students for all of the variations that occur in everyday life? The transfer of skills, also referred to as generalization, must be deliberately taught.

A systematic approach to CBI enables teachers to foresee and plan for as many opportunities as possible for students to apply knowledge. Therefore, the sequential process is not only necessary during teaching, it is crucial to the transfer of skills. Teachers can increase students' proficiency with application skills by utilizing parent input, ongoing assessment, and flexibility in planning. The positive benefits of systematically planning for application skills are evident when students achieve the desired outcomes. Chapter 7 gives detailed plans for systematically approaching maintenance and generalization.

Developmentally Appropriate and Age-Appropriate

For older students, especially those with support needs in middle and high school, the concepts of developmental appropriateness and age-appropriateness sometime seem in conflict.

Beginning with a child's first months of life, adults watch for developmental milestones in the domains of physical growth, gross and fine motor coordination, language acquisition, cognitive development, appropriate social and emotional behavior, and the ability to independently master self-help skills. Parents and teachers know that, for the most part, development is sequential and predictable. Once a young child has progressed through the major accomplishments in these domains, parents and teachers work on increased sophistication and a concentration on academic skills. Only when a child's development does not fit into the broad range of "average" is attention paid to a specific area or areas. When the deficits are obvious or pervasive throughout all domains, teachers or parents identify the need for support. The term *developmental disabilities* describes such pervasive deficits across domains. Developmentally appropriate activities follow a standard sequence; teachers expect students to meet a typical rate of acquisition through to adulthood, when students achieve an acceptable level of mastery.

Age-appropriateness refers to the activities that are typical to a certain age span in children. These averages are broad in nature, but at some point teachers determine that students demonstrate behavior appropriate for their age or that behaviors are immature. A gross oversimplification of this would be seen in the following social activities. Children between 2 and 5 years of age concentrate on playing with manipulative toys, wanting their own way, and using materials to pretend or imagine a self-constructed scenario. In the primary and early elementary years, children enjoy physical games, group activities, organization, rules, and challenges. By middle school, sports, mixed gender activities, and physically challenging games prevail. In high school, young adults make personal choices about their desirable leisure activities and engage in intense relationships. Therefore, a student whose behavior is age-appropriate displays behaviors within the broad ranges just described. A high school student whose behavior is not age-appropriate might play with manipulative toys or engage in imaginative games.

Consider this example. John is a 15-year-old student with extensive support needs. He reads at the first-grade level. When his teacher pulls out yet another book borrowed from the local elementary school, John rebels, "That's baby stuff!" He leaves the room angry and frustrated. It is obvious that the reading material was not age-appropriate despite the fact that it was most likely on John's developmental reading level. John should be reading movie ads, and drug store coupons and looking at pictures in sports or car magazines. When both developmental appropriateness and age-appropriateness are compared to CBI, teachers can construct activities to include both. In the example, the activities are developmentally appropriate because John is asked to read materials that represent his level of reading achievement, and they are age-appropriate because high school students commonly look at advertisements and may be interested in sports or cars.

Problem-Solving

Inevitably students find themselves in situations that differ from their original training. For example, students practice using walk signals to cross the street. When they approach an intersection and the walk sign is out-of-order, what do they do? A teacher is not able to anticipate all of the problems a student might encounter when in the community. Teaching students strategies for dealing with problems is a concerted effort that will assist students as they experience variations within the community. When problems occur under relatively controlled circumstances, teachers can introduce strategies for handling the unknown. Students gain confidence and efficiency by exposure to problem-solving methods prior to being faced with a potentially confusing or dangerous situation.

Continuity Across the Life-Skills Curriculum

It is impossible to plan life-relevant curriculum for all students, including students with support needs, without looking at the entire general education and special education curricula. Despite the arrangement or academic focus, basic skills instruction typically occurs in the classroom. Integrating life-relevant curriculum with basic skills instruction into the whole curriculum makes the best use of classroom time and assures that all areas of the curriculum are being addressed. CBI is an effective method for meeting curricular demands inside and outside the classroom; it enhances teaching continuity and students' ability to generalize skills. The teaching of functional skills and working on IEP objectives are examples of curricular activities that support mastery through instruction in the community. Effective instruction at all levels can be enhanced by activities in a variety of settings that allow repetition and reinforcement of what is taught in classroom environments.

Acceptance in the Community and Local Partnerships

Acceptance goes beyond the philosophy that it is okay for students with or without support needs to use public services. Public reaction to those students is also important. Students with support needs, especially, want to be recognized for the skills they possess. Take the example of Kathy, a young lady with extensive support needs, who wants to buy a stamp. When she enters the post office and steps up to the counter, the postmaster looks at her and says, "You want one stamp, right?" As Ms. Landis, her teacher, later explained to a fellow teacher, "When will they get it? I wanted Kathy to ask to purchase a stamp. She never had the chance to ask. The postmaster spoke for her." It took work on Ms. Landis's part, but in a short amount of time she had asked each proprietor that wanted to be helpful to please say, "May I help you?" as they do with all of their customers, and assume that the students will express their own needs. Acknowledgment of ability extends the concept of acceptance to a more respectful level than the term may imply.

Just as relationships need nurturing, so do partnerships. This is best achieved by demonstrating clear expectations and consistent procedures. As proprietors gain understanding of the goals and approaches used in their places of business, they become comfortable with their roles in the CBI process. Good working relationships help the community at large be informed and involved in the school program. Building activities that foster partnerships provides long-term benefits to students, businesses, and the general public.

How Does CBI Differ From a Field Trip?

Every year Mr. Owens and Ms. Collins take their classes to the local dairy. The students see ice cream being made, watch machines deposit milk in plastic containers, and hear about the aging process of cheese. The students look forward to the trip, bring in money to purchase an ice cream cone, and write a thank-you note when they return to school. This is a field trip.

Ms. Murphy's students make their own lunch every Friday. They plan a well-balanced meal, shop for the items, and prepare the meal. About once a month they have ice cream for dessert. On those days, four students collect money they saved from the class's paper route. They go to the dairy store, bring the ice cream back to school, store it in the freezer, and serve it for dessert. This is an example of CBI.

Community-based instruction is an ongoing instructional process based upon many factors. Transition plans, IEP objectives, family preferences, student interests, and grade level curriculum all have influence on the overall secondary program. Individual students, or small groups receive direct instruction at the actual location they will later use as consumers. The process is continuous, sequential, interactive, and instructive; each intricate step is aimed at achieving students' long-term goals.

Field trips enhance the curriculum by adding an observational and experiential component to specific subjects. Typically field trips are short in duration and are related to a small portion of a unit of study. They occur only occasionally and are attended by one or more classes of students. The goal of a field trip is related to the overall experience of the large group. Individual goals are not considered and personal interaction is minimal.

Field trips are interesting for students of all ages and reflect the school's attempt to enrich the educational experience. Participation in field trips is an inclusive practice that is highly encouraged. Students with disabilities can gain content information, group membership skills, and appropriate behavioral samples from attending field trips with their same-age peers. Nevertheless, the goals for field trips differ from CBI, and the two should not be confused or used interchangeably.

Who Should Participate in CBI?

The secondary school reform movement and the school-to-work initiative provide evidence that all students benefit from participation in activities outside of school. Some of those experiences concentrate on making decisions for postsecondary training and others focus on competitive employment awareness and preparation. Students can make informed decisions about postsecondary training after they gain direct community participation. As for employment, academic and vocational programs, they are enhanced when students are aware of local opportunities and can participate in many types of jobs. CBI enables students to gain independent and semi-independent living instruction in the community, which will prepare them for life after they leave home.

All students who receive special education services through an IEP deserve a secondary program that is aligned with standards, transition planning, and the acquisition of independent living skills. States serve students with disabilities under many labels. Most states design instruction based on student needs rather than a disability label. Fewer states have exceptionality categories and plan instruction to meet identified characteristics of the disability category. States should bypass categorical labels and concentrate on the amount of support required for students to succeed. All secondary students and students with support needs should participate in a curriculum that includes CBI.

The intention is not to separate these two groups of students but to recognize that their programming may differ depending on the intensity of their support needs. Teachers' professional judgment and IEP team planning decisions determine when the delivery of the support occurs within the general program and when it differs from the general education program in frequency, intensity, and by accommodation.

All Secondary Students

It seems that the academic and career planning areas of high school have been the last to encourage community-referenced learning. Only recently have service learning initiatives taken students out of the classroom and into the community to complete a project that contributes to the community's overall well-being. Just as the New American High School initiative recognizes the total community environment for learning, other initiatives encourage community partnerships and learning communities. Not only are community individuals and businesses providing locations in which instruction occurs, they have input into curriculum and offer substantial support. In a similar fashion, some schools are restructuring the large school environment into the concept of learning communities that depict the camaraderie and support of the outside community.

As all students participate in new reforms, they receive portions of their instruction in the community or have community representatives presenting relevant information within schools. Students can now receive special education services and have the opportunity to participate within community partnerships and learning communities. In the long run, added opportunities may lead students to better jobs and broader experiences. Nevertheless, when students' support needs require extensive, long-term exposure and direct interaction in authentic settings to master basic living skills, strategies such as CBI offer the intensity and expansion of locations not possible on the school campus.

Students with Support Needs

Where community-referenced learning broadens the high school program for all students, the use of CBI with students who require special education intervention can greatly increase successful participation in a variety of programs. The intensity of CBI will differ depending on the level of support students need. Students who need intermittent, limited, extensive, or pervasive support can benefit from CBI.

Students with intermittent support needs, or those with mild disabilities, may require help on an as-needed, short-term basis. For example, a young adult with learning disabilities who has a reading disability, yet manages independently in his vocational program, may only need verbal instructions to complete job skills. Academically, this student might use a measurement comparison guide that was designed by a learning facilitator, and may need help highlighting important information in repair manuals. Other than a few adaptations, supports, or prompts, the student with intermittent support needs functions like all other students in the school and community. The community program would provide a list of individuals available to provide minimal support to students upon request.

In another situation, a student has a physical disability and needs small amounts of consistent support over time. The support is not costly and does not require highly specialized staff. Special education professionals help set IEP goals, create transition plans, and monitor the student's progress. Related services such as occupational therapy are provided to help the student use assistive equipment when writing or putting on his coat. Being in a wheelchair adds a mobility challenge, but for this student, minor accommodations are all that are required to perform tasks. The student completes his work in a part-time supported employment environment. For the remainder of the day, he is included in general education classes. With specific instruction in particular areas of need, or by using accommodations to assist the learning process, the student who has limited support needs will require ongoing monitoring and some intervention from special education professionals.

Students with limited support needs, or those with mild to moderate disabilities, have much to gain from participation in CBI. The emphasis may focus on gaining access to postsecondary training, acquiring competitive employment, or managing a household. Regardless of the focus, instruction in the community is directly related to the desired outcome of independence. In addition, self-advocacy skills are a high priority during training. Discerning what help is needed and demonstrating the methods to gain assistance is an important part of transition planning for young adults with limited support needs.

Students with extensive support needs, or those with moderate disabilities, often require direct instruction to acquire functional life skills. These students may exhibit weak academic ability or adaptive skills and behaviors that negatively impact interpersonal relationships. Students with extensive support needs obtain much of their instruction through special education services. Their secondary curriculum concentrates on life skills instruction and vocational training. For example, reading instruction is basic and functional such as reading labels, directions, or job ads. Math skills concentrate on time, money, budget, planning, and problem-solving. Skills needed in entry-level jobs include measuring, following directions, and cooperating with co-workers. The life skills curriculum is emphasized over typical high school subjects. The environments in which extensive support is needed varies from one setting, such as home or work, to many of the locations the student experiences. Students with extensive support needs demonstrate the ability and desire to be independent along with the need for systematic instruction to gain those skills.

Early and continuous participation in the community greatly increases the likelihood that students with extensive support needs will become self-sufficient. Through the use of CBI, teachers infuse concrete skills and problem-solving techniques that ensure independence. These independent living skills may emphasize personal hygiene, time concepts, money management, and interpersonal skills. Community employment experiences stress work-related behaviors and job-related skills. Access to adult services and transportation enable individuals to participate in leisure activities in the community. Each of these experiences improves independence and the quality of life for young adults with extensive support needs.

Students with pervasive support needs, or those with severe disabilities, require intensive intervention to obtain independent skills. The use of adaptive equipment, sophisticated technology, and personal assistants are often necessary to accomplish goals in the areas of personal management and community participation. Students who need pervasive support receive most of their instruction from highly specialized educators. The need for pervasive support makes instruction within the school and throughout the community essential. Using adaptive equipment, arranging transportation, and communicating with related support services personnel, are crucial to students who are striving to reach transition outcomes. Community-Based Instruction is an appropriate method for increasing independence of the students with pervasive support needs.

Just as families expect the school system to ensure independence and community participation for their children with limited or extensive support needs, families of young adults with pervasive support needs want every possible opportunity for their child to function in the community. For some individuals, mastering prerequisite readiness skills is a roadblock to full participation. The acceptance of partial participation allows the student to enter the community early and begin receiving the benefits of community life at a young age. Partial participation, for example, means that although Bill cannot play basketball, he can be a spectator and enjoy a basketball game. Likewise, whether or not Linda can manage money well enough to purchase a new t-shirt, she can shop and choose the t-shirt that she would like to have. Partial participation is an acceptable CBI objective for students who need long-term, intensive support well into adulthood.

Who Are the Stakeholders in CBI?

In a word, everyone! It is impossible to estimate the number of individuals, agencies, and establishments that a person encounters throughout adult life. Students, parents, families, and schools are the immediate stakeholders in CBI. The IEP links the student, family, and school in a partnership which uses CBI to help individual students master independence. Once the student enters the adult world, the supports are reduced and the stakes are higher for both the student and society. Anytime a taxpaying citizen joins the labor market, it reduces the cost for needed financial support or social services. The ultimate stakeholders of CBI, include:

(a) Public service.

(b) Social service agencies.

(c) The general public.

These groups are broad and can be labeled in many ways. Obviously stakeholders represent a huge and varied group that changes with each situation in the student's life and each change in the community.

Public Services

In the broad sense of the term, public services are facilities and establishments open to the general public. These locations in towns and cities include places such as libraries, churches, laundromats, parks, and stores. Establishments benefit when all of their consumers can maneuver and use their services without undue assistance. Consumers typically know what type of product or service they can obtain from a facility, how to access that product, and what is expected from them in the way of behavior, payment, or care of the product. Although the term *service* indicates that a service is provided, in many instances the service is something that is available for the consumer to use independently, such as a laundromat. Public facilities have a commitment that all consumers, including those with disabilities, receive their service in a safe and appropriate manner.

Social Service Agencies

Social services are supported by the taxpaying public and are available, as needed, to anyone. Examples of social services include mental health agencies, employment agencies, residential facilities, and health care centers. With fiscal restraints being the primary challenge to social service agencies, client independence is extremly important. Investments in strategies that increase client independence enable agencies to stretch their resources while serving individuals with disabilities.

General Public

CBI gives students with disabilities the opportunity to learn how to behave appropriately in public. Generally, people as a whole expect to go about their lives with little interference from others. For this to happen, everyone must follow the rules of society, take appropriate care of property, and demonstrate acceptable social behavior. Interaction with people provides natural support and feedback to reinforce the standards of behavior. Everyone must learn how to adjust to the idiosyncrasies of others. Adapting to the personalities of others is a difficult concept that students can learn only by repeated practice and by receiving natural feedback.

What Does the Research and Literature Say About CBI?

Best practices are determined by the results of formal research of teaching methods and the effectiveness of those methods to bring about desired performance outcomes. Practices are perfected and changed as research increases the knowledge base. Teachers who want verification of CBI as a best practice can gain information from practitioners' reports, through research journals, practitioner magazines, and teacher training textbooks. Volumes of information exist about the benefits of ecological approaches to teaching, direct instruction, and community participation in education. Research-based studies and methodology literature support CBI as an instructional strategy.

Research-Based Studies

The majority of CBI research from the past decade looked at students with support needs who received a portion of their educational programs in community settings. Some studies test one particular skill in a specific location. A wealth of research-based studies examine skills related to work performance and behavior. The three studies highlighted below address global topics in specific domains. The first looks at shopping skills over several research projects. The second research study addresses adaptive behavior. The third emphasizes teachers' perceptions of CBI as an instructional method. Classroom teachers typically do not publish the results of their daily activities. Therefore, it is likely that research-based studies are global in scope and reach a broad range of individuals.

In their expansive study about grocery shopping skills for persons with extensive and pervasive support needs, Morse and Schuster (1996) studied 20 different research projects that looked at CBI as a method to teach needed skills to students with disabilities so they could function independently in the community. Comparison of the 20 studies indicated many generalities. The study participants had similar characteristics and the instruction results produced comparable outcomes. Among the most pertinent results were the following items:

Characteristics of participants: Studies typically examined 4 to 10 individuals ranging in age from 8 to 49 years; 60% of those studied were of high school age. The participants' support needs ranged from extensive to pervasive interventions. Most participants received CBI in their secondary programs.

Instruction: The studies focused on different target skills needed for grocery shopping. Generalization, calculator skills, purchasing, and adaptations were emphasized. Methods covered common techniques such as next-dollar strategy, calculator process, picture prompting, task simplification, least-to-most prompting, and unique strategies such as slide simulation. Most participants, 55%, were taught in both the school and community; the remaining 45% were equally split between school-only or community-only settings.

Results: The authors reported that the interventions were successful for all students 96% of the time. Maintenance, generalization, and other research variables were taken into account.

General conclusions: Instruction should begin as early as possible, ideally in elementary grades. In addition, a scaffolding curriculum that frequently revisits topics effectively helped students maintain and generalize skills.

In their study of the impact of CBI on the development of adaptive behavior, McDonnell, Hardman, Hightower, Keifer-O'Donnell, and Drew (1993) reported that the amount of community-based instruction that a student with mental retardation received was a more powerful predictor of gains in adaptive behavior than student's IQ, level of ambulation, or behavioral problems. The authors emphasized that the impact of CBI on the adaptive skills of students with mental retardation was significant. Consequently, these students learned to read situations, problem-solve, and make decisions when they were exposed to the large variety of opportunities in natural environments.

An early study by Westling and Fleck (1991) examined teachers' views of community instruction. They offered several summations about special education teachers' views of CBI and some interesting statistics: Almost 100% of the teachers believed that CBI should be an important part of a public school program. Almost 80% believed that all students with cognitive disabilities have benefited from the use of CBI. When considering duration of instruction, 60% believed that the ideal time for training within a community setting was 1 to 3 hours per week, and 70% felt that one or two students per instructor was ideal for instruction. Not surprisingly, 80% believed that students were more attentive in the community than in the classroom. Teachers believed more preparation on money and language skills and earlier fading techniques were needed. Teachers reported that CBI emphasizes the use of instruction that is more meaningful to students and reduces problems with generalizing skills. Finally, the researchers believed that it is more important for students to know how to adapt to the real world than to acquire academic skills.

It will be interesting to see how school reform movements affect the research on community-referenced learning. Most accountability programs are looking at outcomes of student performance, rather than the process to reach those outcomes. Nonetheless, educators must always consider effective practices that produce positive outcomes. For students with support needs, desired outcomes and specially designed instruction are individual processes. Therefore, alternative forms of assessment, as discussed later, may contain more research-based information about CBI because they look at individual performance. It is clear that there is a need for the collection and interpretation of CBI data.

Methodology Literature

A few themes consistently emerge from the methodology literature used in teacher training programs. First and foremost, teacher training textbooks emphasize the importance of teachers using authentic instructional materials, naturalistic environments, and effective teaching strategies. Special education textbooks are likely to include the importance of learning outside of a classroom. Another significant focus for secondary educators is the need to prepare students to live and work in the community by teaching citizenship and independent living skills and helping students achieve productive employment. Finally, methodology literature stresses the wide range of sequence skills, learning environments, and instructional supports that lead to skill acquisition, generalization, and maintenance.

Methodology literature currently combines a theoretical basis with methods of direct instruction and discovery learning. Educators are expected to create opportunities for spontaneous learning and use supports, such as lists and calculators. Checklists for assessment, tasks for generalization, and self-monitoring and self-correcting strategies describe a few of the techniques promoted as best practices. In the past, Community-Based Instruction appeared to be a strategy promoted in methods courses for use by special education teachers with students requiring intermittent to extensive support. Currently, community-referenced learning is represented in all areas of the secondary curriculum, especially when the targeted outcome is employment.

Perhaps the most significant methodology literature aimed at furthering in-service teachers' skills is the *Life-Centered Career Education* (Brolin, 1997) curriculum. This model outlines a broad view of career stages that span every level of school and early adulthood. Throughout their careers, students are exposed to an ongoing development of awareness, preparation, placement, and follow-up activities. Competency areas, including subcompetency objectives, are detailed and cover a thorough checklist of independent skills implemented by all successful adults. The program systematically supports teachers through content objectives, lesson plans, assessment criteria, and ongoing activities for generalization (see Appendix A).

Methodology articles and training textbooks offer a wide range of support for the use of CBI as an instructional method. Most reports are geared at secondary programs but allude to the premise that community skills may be introduced in the elementary years. There is extensive research occurring in the areas of postsecondary transition and high school reform. Educators have access to the World Wide Web, professional journals, and disability-related organizations that provide substantial literature and encourage active participation in reporting the latest instruction methods. Whether a teacher studies existing research or engages in local long-range studies, research remains a valuable source of the current best practices that are making instructional improvements in the postsecondary lives of high school graduates. In all cases, the benefits of relevancy, independence, confidence, work-related skills, mobility, and participation in society promote the use of community-referenced learning.

Conclusion

Community-Based Instruction is important for many reasons:

1. CBI is ongoing, systematic instruction that takes place in the community.
2. CBI as an instructional method extends students from increased independence to the generalization of skills in many settings.
3. CBI complies with state standards and federal mandates.
4. CBI is not a field trip; it is part of the curriculum, and includes deliberate and frequent assessment.

5. CBI is meant for all students; it represents a strategy to implement school-reform trends that emphasize greater partnerships with and input from community members.

6. CBI supports methods geared at increasing independence for students requiring any level of support.

7. CBI stakeholders are public services, service agencies, and the general public.

8. CBI is noted in research-based studies and methodology literature as an effective practice which increases the likelihood of independence for students with disabilities.

Points to Ponder

1. Why has CBI emerged as an appropriate instructional method for all students in secondary schools?

2. How will the use of CBI support high school reform attempts for all students?

3. How will CBI differ for students with intermittent or limited support needs from that used to increase the independent skills of students with extensive or pervasive support needs?

4. Who are the stakeholders that could see positive results from the use of CBI as a structured part of the secondary program?

5. As with all best practices, there is a research base that emphasizes the tested results of current methods. Who are some of the leaders in promoting data-based verification of CBI as a method to support all students in their quest for professional or occupational training, satisfying careers, and independence?

6. What are some ways to increase participation of parents, advocates, related service providers, and policymakers in the CBI model?

References

Brolin, D.E. (1997). *Life Centered Career Education: A competency based approach* (5th ed.) Arlington, VA: Council for Exceptional Children.

Department of Education. (1992). *Federal Register 34 CFR Parts 300 & 301: Assistance to States for the Education of the Children with Disabilities Program and Preschool Grants for Children with Disabilities: Final Rule. 57*(189), 44804-44815.

Kluth, P., & Straut, D. (2001). Standards for diverse learners. *Educational Leadership, 59*(1), 43-46.

McDonnell, J., Hardman, M.L. Hightower, J., Keifer-O'Donnell, R., & Drew, C. (1993). Impact of community-based instruction on the development of adaptive behavior of secondary-level students with mental retardation. *American Journal on Mental Retardation, 97*, 575-584.

McDonnell, J., Mathot-Buckner, C., & Ferguson, B. (1996). *Transition programs for students with moderate/severe disabilities.* New York: Brooks/Cole.

McDonnell, L.M., McLaughlin, M.J. & Morison, P. (Eds.). (1997). *Educating one and all.* Washington, DC: National Academies Press.

Morse, T.E., & Schuster, J.W. (1996). Grocery shopping skills for persons with moderate to profound intellectual disabilities: A review of the literature. *Education and Treatment of Children, 19,* 487-518.

Sitlington, P.L., Clark, C.M., & Kolstoe, O.P. (2000). *Transition education and services for adolescents with disabilities* (3rd ed.). Boston: Allyn & Bacon.

Turnbull, R., & Cilley, M. (1999). *Explanations and implications of the 1997 amendments to IDEA.* Upper Saddle River, NJ: Merrill.

Wehman, P. (Ed.). (1998). *Developing transition plans.* Austin, TX: Pro-Ed.

Westling, D.L., & Fleck, L. (1991). Teachers' views of community instruction. *Teacher Education and Special Education, 14*(22), 127-134.

Suggested Reading

American Association on Mental Retardation. (1992). *Mental retardation: Definition, classification, and systems of support.* Washington, DC: Author.

Geenen, K. & Ysseldyke, J.E. (1997). Educational standards and students with disabilities. *The Educational Forum, 61.* 220-229.

Sabornie, E.J., & deBettencourt, L.U. (1997). *Teaching students with mild disabilities at the secondary level.* Upper Saddle River, NJ: Merrill.

Snell, M.E., & Brown, F. (2000). *Instruction of students with severe disabilities* (5th ed.). Upper Saddle River, NJ: Merrill.

Wehman, P. (1996). *Life beyond the classroom.* Baltimore: Paul Brookes.

West, L., Leconte, P., King, S., Taymans, J., & Kochlar-Bryant, C. (2000). Comprehensive school reform and students with disabilities. *Benchmarks. The Quarterly Newsletter of the National Clearinghouse for Comprehensive School Reform.*

Westling, D.L., & Fox, L. (2000). *Teaching students with severe disabilities* (2nd ed.). Englewood Cliffs, NJ: Prentice-Hall.

McDonnell, J., Wilcox, B., & Hardman, M.L. (1991). *Secondary programs for students with developmental disabilities.* Boston: Allyn & Bacon.

Chapter 2

Expectations for Community-Based Instruction

> ## In this chapter . . .
>
> ◆ What are the expected outcomes of CBI?
>
> ◆ What are the expectations for students?
>
> ◆ What are the expectations for the family?
>
> ◆ What are the expectations for the community?
>
> ◆ How do the expected outcomes of CBI respond to the school reform issues of standards, assessment, and accountability?

What Are the Expected Outcomes of CBI?

All students expect to leave school prepared for the next step in life. That step may be further vocational training, college, extension of an existing job, or immediate independent living. Regardless of the educational goal, all students want freedom, as well as the ability, to make decisions with support from family, friends, and employers. Students express a desire to apply what they learned in school to the adult world, and they hope for opportunities to earn money. Finally, on the verge of leaving a social-rich environment at the end of their school years, students plan to increase interpersonal contacts and continue a social existence through other endeavors. If students with support needs receive instruction in areas such as travel training, work skills, and leisure choices, their opportunities are greater and their need for specific, individual outcomes is evident. For these reasons, the outcomes of high school transition programs are so interrelated that looking at each area separately causes difficulty, but remains extremely important. The global outcomes of using CBI—including independence, generalization and application of academics, increased opportunities in the job market, and added opportunities for interpersonal relationships—help the school program prepare students for all types of environments. Figure 2.1 represents a hierarchy of expected outcomes of CBI.

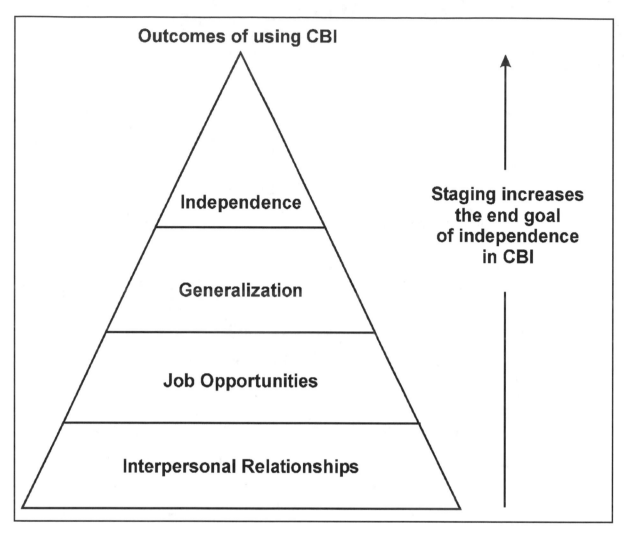

Figure 2.1   Hierarchy of Expected Outcomes of CBI

Independence

Children acquire independence in small increments as they mature. Before children venture beyond their caretakers, they must prove that they are ready to make basic daily decisions without supervision. For example, a student with disabilities who stays at home for 15 minutes, while a parent goes to a convenience store, knows what to do if the phone rings or the television malfunctions. When students with support needs encounter challenges in the community, they get exposure to a complex world of choices, decisions, and problems. They also get supervised practice reacting to the natural occurrences outside of school and home. This exposure enables students to demonstrate appropriate responses to natural dilemmas as they occur, thus proving their ability to manage independently.

Adults believe that their quality of life is directly related to the amount of independence they possess and the ability to make their own choices. Young adults want to be with their friends on shopping trips or other leisure activities. When young adults leave the school system, they want realistic options about living arrangements, employment, and community participation. What is taught through CBI directly affects the possibility that young adults with support needs will have the same opportunities, and autonomy of choices, as other adults, thus allowing them greater independence.

Generalization of Applied Academics

Drill and practice in the classroom supports student acquisition of academic skills. Community-Based Instruction ensures the student's use of acquired academic skills in real-life situations. All areas of postsecondary training, employment, independent living, and leisure activities require the use of basic academic skills. Whether students need instruction in shopping skills, budgeting knowledge, or recreational opportunities, CBI offers experience integrating skills into complex tasks.

Because young adults with limited or extensive support needs have outcomes that highlight further education and employment, the need for academic skills remains paramount. If their postsecondary outcomes include college, young adults have many academic prerequisites. To be accepted in postsecondary college or other academic programs such as apprenticeships, students must have English, science, mathematics, and social studies credits. The general high school program addresses these prerequisite academic areas. Some young adults with extensive or pervasive support needs may go directly into competitive or supported employment. In this case, young adults would use acquired academics to be effective in their jobs. For example, a young adult with support needs who works in a housekeeping position, must follow a checklist, sequence tasks, and evaluate work. Therefore, academic skills taught in the classroom and the community generalize the skills for both situations.

Increased Opportunities in the Job Market

Employment, an ultimate outcome of public education, influences acceptance into adult society. At the same time students learn to maneuver in the community, they can also explore potential work-sites. Face-to-face inquiries help both the student and the employer learn about each other. When young adults secure a job, they begin to build their work-experience portfolio. In addition, they increase their access to resources that will improve their standard of living and expand their social opportunities.

Students who seek, obtain, and retain employment—by demonstrating efficient job skills and appropriate work behaviors—achieve a vital outcome of CBI. Although employment is a transition outcome area in itself, the relationship of CBI and employment are reciprocal. Using CBI as an instructional method adds to students' exposure to the job market and their ability to locate, travel to, and interact within the work setting. Students who are employed gain more opportunities to participate in community activities and achieve social competence. Work experience helps students and their families prepare for future career decisions.

Added Opportunities for Interpersonal Relationships

Community-Based Instruction greatly enhances students' opportunities to interact with other individuals by expanding the environments that they encounter. Virtually everyone relies on family and friends for support in meeting daily needs and facing stress. Just as leaving the classroom and participating in school activities enriches opportunities for friendships, leaving the school building to shop in stores and participate in leisure activities increases the number and diversity of people students encounter.

Teachers must make deliberate efforts to instruct students in locations that attract individuals who are close in age to the students. Teens and young adults utilize recreational facilities, sports activities, clubs, support teams, and youth organizations. The incorporation of these locations into the structured school and community program ensures students' contact with a wide variety of peers, which in turn improves students' work, recreational opportunities, and understanding.

What Are the Expectations for Students?

All students have expectations about what they want to accomplish. States dictate some expectations through standards, while students create other expectations through goals they set for themselves. Goals for all students stem from their desire to independently perform life's daily tasks such as working, managing a home, raising a family, participating in enjoyable activities, and contributing to society. The expectations schools and families place on students create a foundation for lifelong learning and problem-solving. All students have personal expectations for themselves. Figure 2.2 shows a progression of expectations for prominent stakeholders.

Expectations of Stakeholders			
	Preliminary Goal	**Mid-Point Goal**	**Ultimate Goal**
Student:	Master Skills	→ Use Supports Self-Determination	→ Appropriate Behavior
Family:	Communicate	→ Support	→ Follow-Up
Community:	Acceptance	→ Cooperation	→ Support

Figure 2.2   Progession of Expectations for Prominent Stakeholders

Master Skills Necessary for Independence

The concept of independence and the skills needed to achieve independence differ for each individual. Teachers can use a variety of assessment tools to identify specific skills for mastery to enable students to function proficiently on their own.

A purposeful approach to mastering independent skills contains several components:

1. Techniques to help students with support needs in the mastery of skills through classroom activities, described in Chapter 4.

2. Community implementation of acquired skills, described in Chapter 5.

3. Assessment of, and accountability for meeting, students' expectations and outcomes, described in Chapter 6.

Both classroom and community instruction help students function independently through a dynamic process that continually adds more detail to the instruction and broadens students' environment.

Use of Natural Supports, Resources, and Individual Prompts for Independent Functioning

Natural supports are items that are constant in a setting. In school, the natural support to determine lunchtime may be a bell or an announcement. In a restaurant, the natural support may be a hostess who guides the customer to a seat. Resources include assets available to help citizens acquire what they need and want. In a park, the ranger directs patrons to a picnic area or a sign indicates restroom location. Artificial supports, or prompts, aid the individual who needs assistance to function independently. Prompts may include shopping lists, picture directions, or a calculator to determine how much tax will be on an item. Every person uses supports, resources, and prompts to some extent. The goal is to make them as effective and as subtle as possible.

Demonstrate Appropriate Behavior in a Variety of Settings

Most people quickly scan a location and assess the standard of behavior by observing the actions of the people participating in the activities. Dignity and acceptance depend upon the ability to perceive the correct behavior for a setting and perform that behavior consistently. Through CBI, students learn how to interpret and emulate the behavior of people in a setting through direct participation. Unsolicited feedback occurs when other participants include the individual in activities or when they go about their activities without interruption.

Self-Determination

Wehman (2001) defines self-determination as "the capacity to choose and to act on the basis of those choices" (p. 29). He emphasizes that most people develop self-determination as they acquire responsibilities. Wehman also states, "Self-determination requires that the young person be provided with the knowledge, competency, and opportunity necessary to exercise freedom and choice in ways that are valuable to him or her" (p. 29). With the capacity to choose and the knowledge, competency, and opportunity to have a choice, individuals develop greater initiative and ambition, making the concept of self-determination an important component in life. All students want to have choices, make decisions, set goals, and solve problems, even though self-determination is a term used almost exclusively with students who need various levels of support.

Making choices directly relates to understanding preferences. It also gives students the opportunity to experience settings that make different choices available and increase long-term benefits of making choices. For example, choosing between pizza and a hamburger represents a choice; choosing between high-fat content foods and fruits and vegetables allows people to make important life choices. Making minor choices at an early age should prepare students to make major choices later. Decision making works the same way. Where making choices refers to "selecting between alternatives based on individual preferences" (p. 45), decision making involves incorporating steps that consider alternatives, consequences, importance, and values of an action (Wehman, 2001).

Problem-solving and goal setting represent different entities. Problem-solving indicates a situation that needs to be corrected for life to run smoothly. Goal setting implies a long-term process of stating a plan, listing objectives, implementing strategies, evaluating the process, and refining the process. The evaluation of the process that follows goals is measured by the attainment of the goal (Wehman, 2001).

Students are expected to participate in the educational planning process. In planning for transition, the goals extend from educational goals to making plans for life. Because the process of self-determination changes constantly, individuals with support needs can greatly increase their skills through activities taught and perfected using CBI. This makes self-determination perhaps the most important of all expectations. Not only do students make major life decisions, they plan for the future and initiate progress toward achieving increased self-fulfillment.

What Are the Expectations for the Family?

Typical family activities provide the natural setting for students with disabilities to practice community skills. To families' credit, many students receiving support services have been to shopping centers, grocery stores, and recreation sites throughout their childhood years. Schools encourage families to continue those activities on a regular basis. The family's increased involvement through open communication, supportive activities, and follow-up activities adds practical experience that is crucial to the teen and young adult years.

Communicate With the School

The family—including the young adult receiving services, parents, guardians, caretakers, siblings, friends, and extended family members—has a responsibility to communicate with school frequently. Communication may be initiated by anyone at any time. Schools usually initiate communication through formal or informal notes, questionnaires, planning meetings, newsletters, and phone calls. Families may be hesitant to initiate communication until they feel comfortable and included. Effective communication must be two-way, frequent, and most often, informal. The family who gives frequent input and receives feedback will have a clear picture of shared goals and responsibilities for the young adult in any type of high school program.

Support the School Program

A concrete level of support begins to form when the family demonstrates to the secondary student their mutual interest in the entire school program and their hopes for the student's progress. When families return signed permission forms promptly and stay abreast of activities, schools are saved from making repeated requests for papers and materials. If students have a checklist of items needed for an activity, the family can help by reviewing the list with the student and ensuring that the student is prepared for the day. For example, if a young adult is going to a fitness center, a family can help a student choose the most comfortable clothing for the day, which is helpful to the teacher. Minimal financial support, help with a fundraiser, and volunteering enhance activities and assist the school in providing a quality program.

Continue the Process at Home

Acknowledging a student's progress and offering an opportunity to demonstrate acquired skills greatly enhances the individual's competence and confidence. The family may provide follow-up experiences in similar locations to those taught in school or introduce the young adult to other community locations normally not accessible at school. Students' participation levels increase when they can participate independently in neighborhood activities. Figure 2.3 indicates the relevant activities with the family to reinforce the school program in a less formal, more enjoyable way.

Areas you can work on at home with a young adult to "bridge" what they are learning in school to activities done at home.

1. Make calls to find out movie times or set up appointments.

2. Locate items at the store that you need through coupons or a small written list. Include some items she has not previously located.

3. Incorporate problem solving techniques into problems encountered at home. Identify the problem, the cause, and help think of possible solutions.

4. Give a "To do" list that must be accomplished throughout the week.

5. The next time you go to a restaurant: A. Read a menu B. Order a meal, and C. Figure out the appropriate tip using the tip chart.

   When eating out, keep in mind a financial limit that may be spent on a meal, have the young adult calculate the tax and tip into the total order.

Figure 2.3   Relevant activities with the family to reinforce the school program in a less formal, more enjoyable way.

What Are the Expectations for the Community?

The community, specifically the people in the community who run businesses and public services, contribute to the CBI program by accepting all patrons and cooperating with on-site training in natural and supportive ways. The expectations from the community differ little from what is expected by the general public, but that may not be obvious to employees who manage and staff businesses. Careful planning and clear communication emphasizing established practices and typical results create a long-lasting relationship that serves all citizens with little attention to learning or physical differences.

Demonstrate Acceptance

Laws such as the Americans with Disabilities Act (ADA) grant physical accessibility into places of business and public facilities. Personal acceptance occurs gradually as individuals with support needs live in their home communities. Schools may initiate visitations as one way for acceptance to occur, but it would be more natural to learn about each other in the actual setting—the store or business targeted for training. By allowing training within their businesses, owners and managers take the opportunity to know more about young adults in general and specifically about young adults receiving specialized instruction. This leads to community acceptance of the students and increases students' independence opportunities more than visitations or awareness activities could.

Cooperate With On-Site Training Procedures

The community's role is an important part of setting up a CBI program, as described in Chapter 3. Teachers should not assume that store managers or service providers will know the expected outcomes and methods used to promote independence in students with disabilities. It is the school's responsibility to thoroughly explain the training process to community members. Once that exchange has occurred, proprietors and employees will be aware of their roles in the CBI program. The store employee can contribute to the on-site success of CBI by doing the following:

- Greet the student when she or he enters a site.
- Provide store maps and layouts.
- Allow extra time for students to count out money.
- Encourage student independence, withholding assistance until requested.
- Assist the student when asked.

Most business locations already provide the above services for all customers. Reinforcing those actions that occur naturally increases employees' confidence and exemplifies acceptance of all patrons.

How Do the Expected Outcomes of CBI Respond to the School Reform Issues of Standards, Assessment, and Accountability?

A simple reply to this question would be to say that standards include items that all students need to master in order to perform daily activities in all aspects of their lives. Another answer might imply that standards represent the opportunity to learn, especially for individuals with support needs, which directly relates to CBI outcomes. Neither of these responses thoroughly explains the three issues stated in the question. Standards, assessment, and accountability are interrelated, yet each addresses a piece of the reform movement affecting the education of all students. Approaching these reform issues in a comprehensive manner meets both the intent of the reform and the inclusion of all students in an effective educational process.

Standards. Standards cover four areas: Content, performance, opportunity to learn, and assessment. According to Ysseldyke (1994), content standards describe the specific knowledge and skills that students acquire as a result of exposure to the curriculum. Performance standards indicate the level of competence that must be attained and the quality of student performance. Opportunity-to-learn standards imply the conditions that establish achievement of standards, or accountability. Finally, assessment standards provide guidelines for testing achievement. CBI outcomes relate to content standards in social studies areas, for example, that discuss managing money, functioning in the community, and developing personal relationships. Assessment standards stress the use of authentic and performance-based assessment geared to measure the generalizability of skills. Generalized skills are also highly represented in strategies that encourage the use of CBI.

An oversimplification of what the standards require could include a statement such as, "comprehensive content and effective performance demonstrated by all students." McDonnell, McLaughlin, and Morison (1997) set out to correlate the complicated standards-based reform movement to the instruction of students with support needs. They charged the Committee on Goals 2000 and the Inclusion of Students with Disabilities to compare special education policies and practices as they relate to standards-based reform. According to McDonnell et al., "There is a scarcity of research evidence directly bearing on the effects of standards-based reform, much less their impact on students with disabilities" (p. 2). Despite this challenge, the committee offered assumptions about standards and made recommendations based upon what they discovered by comparing existing policy and proposed reform. They addressed questions such as: "Should students with disabilities be included in standards-based reform? How do standards affect the postschool outcomes required in transition planning? And, how will students with disabilities be assessed to determine that they are meeting the standards?"

One item made evident by the committee was that "all students should have access to challenging standards and that policy makers and educators should be held publicly accountable for every student's performance" (McDonnell et al., p. 2). The committee continued "if standards-based reform is part of a state's general education framework, students with disabilities should have access to the relevant curriculum and assessment" (McDonnell et al., pp. 3-4). The rationale behind those statements emphasizes that, by being part of the standards, students with support needs should receive the instruction needed to meet those standards. Also, the committee recommended incentives that excluded students needing support, because they reflected negatively on the school's overall results, be eliminated. The challenge of including students with support needs in standards remains obvious. How do educators accommodate for individual needs and provide services that will afford students with disabilities access to the general curriculum and ensure their success in standardized assessment?

Standards-based reform influences student outcomes. Secondary schools traditionally promote vocational/employment outcomes for students with support needs. Standards go beyond employment to promoting outcomes that include literacy, productive citizenship, and personal satisfaction. McDonnell et al. (1997, p. 2), point out that, "The emphasis on post-school outcomes has shaped the curricular and instructional experiences of many students with disabilities." They questioned whether states would adopt vocational/career standards and how those standards might affect students with support needs.

Life skills taught through CBI can blend with standards if states and districts acknowledge the curricular process and positive outcomes that can be gained from this reform. If educators develop ways to help students meet standards in relation to individual goals stated on students' IEPs, there is a possibility that a direct correlation between instruction and standards will occur. McDonnell, et al. state, "the pedagogical methods incorporated into many state standards emphasize active learning, group projects with high cognitive demands, and students 'constructing' knowledge from various experiences and informed sources" (p. 6). This statement echoes the CBI description in this book. Ultimately, state legislation which outlines how life skills instruction and CBI will blend with standards is needed. Districts need to commit to accomplishing state mandated guidelines. These factors indicate that life skills instruction, using CBI, is compatible with state standards.

Assessment. The marriage of standards and assessment is highly publicized. Assessment is the mode used to judge the accountability of public schools. According to McDonnell et al., the public accountability of general education is different from the IEP-based evaluation system used in special education. Furthermore, many states do not require that students with support needs participate in standardized testing, which then excludes them from the accountability system. To increase participation of students with support needs in the accountability system, many states have allowed minor accommodations for students to complete the assessment.

As states experiment with pilot programs to develop alternative assessment for students with support needs, creative forms of measuring student achievement are emerging. Special education has long prided itself in evaluating students by means other than paper-pencil, norm-based tests. Designing an assessment, complete with generic accommodations, diverges from the individualization movement that created the current system. Of course, individuals with support needs, their families, educators, and advocates have fought hard to guarantee equal access to all opportunities. If equal access to standards and assessment means equal access to education, the discipline will develop the necessary alternative assessments to continue those ideals. Until ecological assessment is more widely used as a performance indicator for all students, the skills learned through Community-Based Instruction will have to be thoroughly documented to show the accountability associated with this and all authentic experiences.

This discussion addresses large-scale, annual standardized assessment for the purpose of meeting state accountability requirements. Most assessments that teachers perform are considered informal assessments related to student progress and teacher effectiveness on an individual and personal level. Chapter 6 offers several examples of informal assessment, such as checklists, rubrics, and discussion about portfolio artifacts.

Accountability. Accountability issues offer proof that students reach their educational goals and that interventions and support systems are working. Maybe the question is not, "How do the expected outcomes of CBI correspond to accountability?" but "How do teachers apply accountability concepts to CBI outcomes?" Surely, the overall expected outcomes are for all students to reach their goals, perform skills independently in the community, and carry the acquired skills into other environments. The typical student's accountability is assessed through state standardized tests. The accountability of students with support needs receiving adapted curricula is measured by collected data that indicates if outcomes have been met. The biggest challenge for students with support needs, in respect to the use of CBI, is not showing evidence that students have reached their goals. Instead, it is making sure that standards are incorporated into the students' IEPs and that assessment indicates the student's performance in relation to those standards. Linking standards and specially designed instruction is a challenging step to promote inclusionary practices and functional programming for all students. Individual state legislatures mandate standards and assessments, which determine if students achieve the desired standards. Young adults with support needs, parents, educators, and advocates must have representation in the decision-making process as states revise and develop new standards. Important stakeholders and advocates for students with support needs can encourage states to solve the problems associated with meeting individual needs within generic frameworks. Community-Based Instruction represents one strategic method to achieve lifelong independence. Creating a curriculum that uses functional programming to meet standards in least-restrictive and most-supportive environments is an ongoing goal of IDEA '97.

Conclusion

Expectations and outcomes for all secondary students are distinct to the individual yet relate to what society expects of all citizens. Expectations and outcomes are determined by needs, interests, and input from a variety of entities. The emphasis must be on an optimistic vision and mutual involvement of all stakeholders—the individual, family members, school, and community. Outcomes are not driven by the challenge to meet them or the available resources; they are developed with the future independence of the individual as the primary goal. Case Study 2.1 relates how expectations and self-determination affect student outcomes.

No discussion about expectations and outcomes is complete without considering standards, assessment, and accountability issues. It is important to use all three to improve the education of all students. The dilemma of how to include all students, especially students with support needs, has not been completely solved. However, the motivation to have all students improve their skills is the primary interest of all stakeholders. Nevertheless, designing appropriate outcomes and goals relies upon the collaborative efforts of all participants.

Case Study 2.1

A popular high school student was critically injured in an assault just outside of the school-yard. After much rehabilitation, he returned to school for 3 years. He received many services including special education, physical therapy, and direct family and vocational counseling. Over the 3 years, he progressed to the point that he was physically independent and cognitively able to manage basic skills. The transition team planned for him to receive vocational training and independent living skills through two adult agencies, which were aimed at supporting individuals with similar challenges.

As is often the case, a few years after exiting the school system, the follow-up team was unable to locate this young man. It was unfortunate because there had been much effort and anticipation put into his plan. Five years after the student graduated, one of the transition team members was visiting a community several hundred miles from the school. An article about the young man, his fiancé, their favorite pastime, and their future plans was featured in the local paper. Although this is not the way the school system had planned to assess their long-term outcomes, the student met his goals of independence and self-determination in textbook fashion.

Points to Ponder

1. What positive outcomes can be expected when CBI is used as a consistent component of a secondary program?

2. What results can secondary students with support needs, or their families, expect from using CBI as a strategy during their high school programs?

3. How do local communities benefit from assisting schools in promoting CBI in their local businesses?

4. How do the outcomes achieved through the use of CBI support accountability issues?

5. How can schools better track transition students after graduation?

References

McDonnell, L.M., McLaughlin, M.J., & Morison, P. (Eds.). (1997). *Educating one and all.* Washington, DC: National Academies Press.

Wehman, P. (2001). *Life beyond the classroom* (3rd. ed.). Baltimore: Paul H. Brookes.

Ysseldyke, J.E., & Others (1994). *Students with disabilities and educational standards: Recommendations for policy and practice.* Minneapolis: University of Minnesota, National Center on Educational Outcomes. (ERIC Document Reproduction Service No. ED 372 561).

Suggested Reading

Beakley, B.A., & Yoder, S.L. (1998). Middle schoolers learn community skills. *TEACHING Exceptional Children, 30*(3), 12-18.

Brolin, D.E. (1997). *Life centered career education: A competency based approach* (5th ed.). Arlington, VA: Council for Exceptional Children.

Csapo, M. (1991). Community-based instruction: Its origin and description. In D. Baine (Ed.), *Instructional environments for learners having severe handicaps.* (ERIC Reproduction Service No. ED 344 389).

Edgar, E., & Polloway, E. A. (1994). Education for adolescents with disabilities: Curriculum and placement issues. *Journal of Special Education, 27*, 438-452.

Gandal, M., & Vranek, J. (2001). Standards: Here today, here tomorrow. *Educational Leadership, 59*(1), 7-13.

Glatthorn, A.A., & Craft-Tripp, M. (2000). *Standards-based learning for students with disabilities.* Larchmont, NY: Eye On Education, Inc.

McDonnell, J., Wilcox, B., & Hardman, M.L. (1991). *Secondary programs for students with developmental disabilities.* Boston: Allyn & Bacon.

Sale, P., & Martin, J.E. (1997). Self-determination. In P. Wehman, J. Kregel, & P. Wehman, (Eds.), *Functional curriculum for elementary, middle, and secondary age students with special needs.* Austin, TX: Pro-Ed.

Sitlington, P.L., Clark, G.M., & Kolstoe, P.P. (2000). *Transition education and services for adolescents with disabilities* (3rd ed.). Boston: Allyn & Bacon.

Chapter 3

Developing Procedures to Implement Community-Based Instruction

In this chapter . . .

- ◆ What basic challenges face the implementation of CBI?

- ◆ What 10 steps are essential to utilizing CBI as an instructional strategy?

- ◆ What are appropriate CBI sites for students between ages 18 and 21?

- ◆ What resources are needed to support CBI?

- ◆ What support systems are needed to make CBI successful?

- ◆ How are support systems developed?

- ◆ How are community partnerships developed?

What Basic Challenges Face the Implementation of CBI?

It makes sense to instruct students of all ability levels in the settings that best serve their acquisition of standard-based content and individual goals. The procedure used to implement any instructional strategy requires reflective examination of the benefits and expected challenges that occur. Educators usually promote the positive aspects of a method first and then interject the issues to problem solve. Ideally, the benefits of CBI will be well established and possible challenges will be identified and researched prior to the implementation of CBI. When all steps are in place progress will not be hindered or delayed by possible challenges. Two distinct issues need explanation. One involves local philosophy and practice, the other hardcore logistical issues. First, implementing CBI for all students in inclusive settings occurs with painstaking effort. That is not to say that some students, due to the intensity of support needs, may still require more individualized programs. Second, transportation, liability, and general insurance issues represent higher-level administrative concerns that directly affect teachers' and immediate supervisor's accomplishments in using CBI in the general and specialized curriculum.

Implementing CBI for all Students in Inclusive Settings

This guidebook looks at the benefits of all students receiving instruction in the community. When considering inclusive practices, we typically think of a student that has support needs. Families, teachers, school districts, and states embrace the best practice of teaching students with support needs through the general curriculum. What seems to be a natural phenomenon to society has challenged schools for many years. One controversy about the use of CBI is that it represents the "pull-out" model, which appears contrary to inclusive programming. However, CBI depicts specially designed instruction based upon individual needs, and should not hinder the use of inclusive practices or least restrictive environments as mandated by IDEA '97. The community that the students enter has a natural proportion of individuals with support needs, which highlights the value of the method. The location of instruction used in CBI prepares the student for a more inclusive adult life than they might have achieved without CBI.

Students and families must state their needs and preferences whenever goals and transition outcomes are discussed. Grade level and ability level influence the curricular focus throughout the years the student is in school. In the elementary grades, a developmental approach to teaching basic skills and academics represents a large part of the curriculum. Students with intermittent and limited support needs maintain an academic concentration until graduation or beyond. By middle school, students with extensive or pervasive needs begin to switch their emphasis to independent living skills, using CBI as a primary method of meeting goals. These students often focus on employability skills by high school. Students' priorities are determined based on the expected direction they plan after graduation.

The challenge with all curricula remains getting every subject, all necessary content, and relevant experiences within the confines of a school year. Families and professionals spend an abundance of time with the student. School personnel and related services prioritize the curricula and set expectations, plan content, and set timelines. Effective planning ensures that the most important interests, preferences, and skill areas are achieved by graduation. Ultimately, the student and family, with the advice of experienced professionals, decide where, what, and how learning should occur. Since students' interests and preferences change as they mature, most teachers, counselors, and caseworkers recommend a well-rounded program covering all areas of instruction and emphasizing decision-making and problem-solving over a high concentration of one specific subject. Setting priorities which are flexible enough to meet students' needs and interests becomes a dynamic process when educators maintain focus on stated outcomes and the processes needed to reach IEP goals.

The best placement for the young adult with support needs continues to be in the local high school. Scheduling should allow for double periods to be devoted to CBI as they would a science with a laboratory or a family and consumer science class. Some high schools have gone to intensive scheduling, which gives each class about 90 minutes per period. Scheduling one or two of those time blocks in a week could accommodate using CBI to meet IEP goals.

Another option would be to use the local career and technical center. The center allows for more movement than the general high school, plus, it has the added benefits of employment, and some may have home living facilities on site. Daily scheduling in career/technical schools often fall into two forms of arrangements. One setting offers a half-day in high school followed by the student traveling to the career/technical center. Another setting includes a comprehensive career/technical school that offers the high school and career/technical programs in one building. Either arrangement would be favorable for meeting the transition needs of students with intermittent and limited support needs who are between the ages of 16 to 21. As those students acquired the career skills needed for their chosen fields and engage in employment opportunities outside of the career/technology center, they would have an opportunity to practice CBI skills needed for employment. In rare incidences a career/technology center will house a few classes to serve high school students with extensive or pervasive support needs. In these cases, there may be independent living settings or locations to practice basic occupational skills among peers their age.

The opportunity to have peer support or student volunteers accompany students on CBI trips is readily available in both the high school and technical center. All participants benefit from the instruction and variety of locations visited outside the school building. Long- and short-range planning that involves general education teachers, special education teachers, parents, and administrators, ensures a systematic and structured CBI program that can increase interaction among all students, support student learning, and accomplish IEP goals.

Transportation and Insurance Issues

A school district's administration provides support by supplying clearly stated liability information and cooperating with schools on transportation issues. Liability insurance covers the student, in the event of an injury while participating in CBI, and property damage, in case a student destroys a product or display in a business. Both of these circumstances are unlikely, but possible. A teacher is not in the position to provide this coverage. Personal insurance rates would skyrocket if teachers transported students in their own vehicles. Part of the district's responsibility is to acknowledge and provide liability insurance to the extent that they feel is adequate. IDEA '97 includes transportation of students for IEP implementation.

Insurance issues demand careful scrutiny. District insurance carriers need precise details about the age of students who participate in off-campus activities and the distance from school they travel to receive instruction. Insurance carriers also need complete and honest information about health or behavioral issues. Even with this information, carriers may dictate strict guidelines that are directly related to transportation needs. Some districts contract with their transportation providers for all transportation services, in which case travel insurance would be covered by the provider. Some districts own vans for use by small groups. Regardless of the mode of transportation or other possible liability issues in the community, insurance carriers' instructions must be followed by supervisors and teachers.

A comprehensive program also includes a transportation budget. Only a small portion of schools are within a safe walking distance of community training sites. As mentioned earlier, some districts have a vehicle that may be used to provide transportation to and from training sites. Because CBI is best implemented in small groups, a school bus is not always the most appropriate means of transportation.

Arranging transportation requires more than just scheduling a ride; it includes all classes that attend activities more than a mile from school. CBI scheduling may compete with sports, dramatics, clubs, and job training for transportation. Paraprofessionals can request help scheduling transportation from clerical personnel.

CBI planners should also consider public transit. If available, this is a good opportunity to expand the young adults' skills. There are also costs associated with public transportation. The Americans with Disabilities Act has mandated accommodations and access, but availability and cost vary greatly according to the community size and resources. Teaching students how to read mass transit schedules and follow maps adds another valuable dimension to the instructional process. Unfortunately, the use of public transportation, except in large cities, cannot be customized to meet individual educational needs. Nevertheless, if public transit is identified as a major goal area of instruction, then the skills needed for successful public travel become part of the CBI plan.

What 10 Steps Are Essential to Utilizing CBI as an Instructional Strategy?

Schools, that are initiating or want to improve the use of CBI, could use the following list as a guide to creating a comprehensive instructional plan, which considers students' needs and preferences, family input, individualized planning, community location, and administrative support. The sequence of steps is deliberate. However, steps may overlap or occur at different time intervals. The overall process is important, and the specific steps within the process will depend on the district's background experience and immediate need. Demographics and local philosophy influence every aspect of curriculum and instructional methodology. Expect to include local needs or direct attention to one area more than others to meet individual needs. A list of suggested steps in developing a CBI program include the following:

1. Communicate with students and parents.
2. Conduct an ecological inventory.
3. Plan for individuals.
4. Acquire school support.
5. Develop curriculum.
6. Create a master plan.
7. Plan instruction.
8. Research locations.
9. Teach and assess in the classroom, school, and community.
10. Evaluate the process based on student performance.

1. Communicate with students and parents.

Communication with families should be an ongoing process from both the classroom teacher and the school. As pertaining to CBI, communication should begin with a notice that the school will be performing an ecological survey; this will give the student and family a preliminary view of the importance of the actual survey which will follow shortly thereafter (see Appendix B1). Throughout the process several types of formal and informal communication devices are developed to encourage ongoing dialogue about students. Brief notes serve to keep everyone informed about events and activities occurring inside and outside of school. Educators should use formal means of sharing—newsletters and flyers—to keep parents informed about school activities. One example of how to share basic information about CBI excursions is through a class newsletter (see Appendix B2). Another example would be a once-a-year parent handbook that discusses the process of using CBI as an instructional method (see Appendix B3).

Increase student independence by making the student responsible for the materials needed in school. Instruct the students in the use of a planner, an appointment book or calendar, in which they write down their schedules. Students benefit from this instruction by coming to school prepared for the activities of the day and by seeing all of their activities in an organized fashion. This skill also applies to other areas of daily living. Later, instruction in e-mail and the use of Web pages may also increase the students' abilities to function independently.

Send informal messages to families, supervisors, and businesses reminding all stakeholders of coming events. A not-so-subtle reminder to parents is the official permission slip (see Appendix B4). Teachers suggest that one permission slip be used to cover all of the travel to community sites, instead of repeatedly asking for permission each time students leave the school building. Keep a supervisor informed of classroom activities on a regular basis. Contact store managers by student-made flyers, or send thank-you notes and reminders of the next visit. Ultimately, when the strategy of instructing students in the community is nonintrusive, the need for written communication is replaced by verbal interaction.

2. Conduct an ecological inventory.

One of the first steps in the CBI process is an ecological inventory that identifies student and family desires for the student. The inventory looks at specific environments and sub-environments that the student accesses, identifies the activities and tasks in each of the sub-environments, then uses the information to compare the environments with the types and numbers of environments in which same-age peers participate. Future environments that the student and family want to emphasize during transition planning can be included on the survey. Ecological inventories are available commercially or may be teacher-made to match a specific region. Often more than one inventory is needed to address different areas of the transition plan. Inventories may address specific areas, such as academic needs or career interests, or they may check specific skills and family preferences (see Appendix B5).

3. Plan for individuals.

Because CBI is a strategy that enhances the curriculum for all students, the need for individual planning may be minimal. The individual plan for any student will depend on several of the following factors: the amount of instruction that can be accomplished within general education settings, the current age of the student, prerequisite skills, longterm outcomes, family involvement, and natural and community supports. Planning for students with support needs occurs through the development of the transition portion of the IEP, when student and family needs and interests are assessed and recorded. Outcomes are stated for the transition plan, which then drive the IEP goals. The IEP team establishes the transition outcomes, IEP goals, and benchmarks. The CBI method can be used to meet the benchmarks. When the goals for each student are established, teachers can determine the collective needs of all students and begin outlining the strategies that will address the important goals for the entire class and the individual students.

4. Acquire school support.

School support begins with the immediate supervisor or principal and continues to the school board. Present the school board, administrators, and staff with facts about the purposes and outcomes of CBI and how the use of this method improves instruction, addresses standards, and accomplishes accountability. It is important that school boards and administrators not simply understand and encourage the CBI process, they must also grant written permission for the activities to occur. In settings that use community-referenced learning for all students, support may occur in school reform issues already directed by the school board. In some districts, when official permission is granted, transportation and financial supports naturally follow. In other districts, the philosophy and recognition of the method are embraced, however the financial support must be determined. A district-level permission slip may be used that would show the overall acceptance of the process (see Appendix B6).

Financially supporting CBI may extend beyond the school board. In a climate that has many school factions competing for a limited amount of fiscal resources and accountability issues driving the curriculum, there is a need for creative planning to support CBI. Supervisors and teachers may seek funds from community and corporate donors to supplement the school curriculum budget. Personal letters may be used to secure funds and supplements for the program. Schools also support the CBI program by granting permission for special projects. Some schools sponsor fundraisers. Others are wary of using traditional fundraisers because they appear to be charity events for students requiring extensive and pervasive support. The solicitation of outside contributions may assist the CBI process, but the ultimate responsibility for implementing the strategy lies within the school system (See Appendix B7).

5. Develop curriculum.

Transition plans for students requiring support should focus on the general education curriculum for all students. As much of the curriculum as possible should be taught in the general classroom. How much of a student's instructional experience occurs outside of the general classroom depends on the student's ability to generalize classroom learning into his or her own environments; student age and ability also affect this. As students get older, they receive proportionally more of their instruction in the community. A curriculum for students with limited support needs is a comprehensive and thorough combination of skills needed for postsecondary planning, employment, independent living, and community participation. A curriculum for students with extensive needs will apply curricular components through functional activities and practical experiences using modifications and adaptations in the community. Examples of modifications and adaptations are shown in figure 3.1.

• Assistive technology • Block scheduling • Break multistep problems into smaller, more manageable chunks • Carbon paper note-taking by peer • Classroom behavior management system • Community-based instruction • Do not grade for spelling or grammatical errors • Drill and practice • Extra time for tests/quizzes • Functional academics	• Hands-on activities • Highlighting material • Individual instruction • Individualized behavior management system • Lecture notes provided for student • Limited distractions • Limited number of objectives for general education classes • Multisensory instruction • No written/essay tests or quizzes • One-to-one assistant • Oral tests • Peer buddy	• Positive feedback and reinforcement • Proximity seating • Repeated practice • Small group instruction • Tests/quizzes taken in support room for general education classes • Use of calculator • Use of computer • Use of graphic organizers • Use of manipulatives • Use of prompting • Use of word banks • Writing on every other line

Figure 3.1 Examples of Modifications and Adaptations

With the overall curriculum in place for all students, teachers can look at the needs of the students who require support and develop a sequential plan. Possible sequential steps for curricular planning will help the teacher think through a comprehensive design aligned with standards, accountability issues, and the demands of IEPs. As with all areas of curriculum and program planning, the scope and sequence of skills is a fluid list that allows new environments to be added and other locations revisited. Other teachers, mentors, curriculum specialists, and commercial material provide support for curriculum development.

6. Create a master plan

A master plan, which integrates the general education curriculum and a systematic approach to CBI, is developed through painstaking consideration of the needs of all students. Standards, the accountability process, the established needs for all adults to live independently, and the community input that has been gathered from families, employers, and local businesses will affect the plan. Teachers should try to create a master plan that combines the school's mission, the entire curriculum, the goals of students and families, and the recommendations of the stakeholders. The master plan should be sequential but subject to individualization. The more consistency across curricular areas, the more practical the plan will be when adding the community components for individual students.

Creating a daily, weekly, and monthly schedule will be a dynamic process that incorporates the assessment plan, school calendar, district policy, program directives, and fiscal matters. The plan should begin with a general outline of outcomes and add individual goals, locations, and timeframes. The plan should allow flexibility when indicating classroom activities, community activities, and home or follow-up activities. Broad details that apply to every student can be augmented by specific details that surface with individual students. The master plan is a multiyear process that factors in the age and ability levels of all students. A workable master plan will change as new initiatives surface and will always be in a state of development.

7. Plan instruction.

Instruction occurs in every educational experience, in most cases the general education classroom. However, for students with extensive or pervasive needs, a separate classroom is used. At first glance, it seems that the ideal arrangement for CBI would be to have the classroom directly in the community 100% of the time. That is not appropriate for students under 18 years of age, or those who generalize easily. Participation in school activities generates the most interaction with age-peer models and age-appropriate activities. Careful planning ensures that academics, social behaviors, and skills needed to function independently are addressed across the curriculum and in all learning environments. Therefore, teachers need to determine, by degree of need, which students respond best to classroom instruction and which should receive frequent instruction in the community.

Instruction should introduce and reinforce basic academic, language, math-related, and social skills in the classroom. Students and teachers can problem-solve and make decisions in the quiet and safe confines of the school as well. Role-playing, peer support, and graduated prompting also occur in the classroom. On the days when instruction occurs in the community, teachers should continue instruction at the student's current level of proficiency. If a situation occurs that requires direct instruction, teachers conduct that instruction on site. If the student demonstrates effective skills, educators can provide feedback immediately. Ideally, the instructional process will be so adaptable and fluid that the location of instruction is not an issue and students are comfortable in all settings, especially in the community.

All lessons need objectives, materials, procedures, and assessments as a basic core of the plan. Lessons need to include a logical sequence, a clear description of teacher-guided or discovery learning, and extensive opportunities for student practice. A consistent format for planning will also help students recognize the learning process in which they are a part and help them anticipate and implement behaviors that are required with each activity. There are many opportunities for a teacher to add appeal and creativity to the design throughout CBI once the basic planning is accomplished (see Appendixes B8, 9).

8. Research locations.

It is important for a teacher to recognize the many variables that determine the type of locations needed to implement CBI strategies. Information gained from the ecological inventory will provide useful data. Finally, information from families and people in the community will aid teachers' selection of instructional locations. Standards, accountability issues, and the outcomes discussed at transition and IEP meetings should be considered. The types of businesses and recreational facilities mentioned are more important than the identification of specific sites. However, for students with pervasive support needs, specific locations may be chosen to reduce the amount of generalization activities required. The research process enables teachers to judge what locations are feasible for the school to utilize on a frequent basis and those locations that are unique to individual students because they require specialized transportation or added expense. Finally, the overall curriculum will determine which locations address the independent needs of all students and support the requirements of state standards.

A variety of categorical sites are essential to the overall CBI process. Locations should include places that the typical person frequents weekly, such as grocery stores, drug stores, department stores, and leisure establishments. Sites that are diverse enough to allow for generalization among the categories, yet common enough to be manageable within the curriculum should be included. Also include locations visited by the typical person on an infrequent basis, but that are important to an individual's total independence, such as doctors' offices, movie theaters, parks, and local vacation sites.

Once the type of training site is established, scrutiny of the characteristics of the specific location is helpful. Sites that are easily accessible to school and physically accessible for all students are ideal. Locations that are organized in a manner that allows for some consistency in locating items, chain stores for example, work well for CBI. On the other hand, local stores usually have fewer changes in displays and less staff turnover. In addition, it is important to feel that the site is a clean and safe learning environment for students (see Appendix B10).

In deciding which locations should be used, the teacher must observe the characteristics of the staff. The support of the management is crucial to success. Managers who understand the CBI process and instruct their employees to cooperate with the process support the school program immensely. Since CBI represents an instructional practice, employees need to know that students will be removing and replacing items from shelves to practice specific skills. As stated in Chapter 2, employees need instruction about their role. They should be naturally helpful, but not overly indulgent of the student. Friendly establishments not only cooperate and assist the school program, they also indicate to the young adult that their patronage is desired and important to the business.

Classroom teachers can plan on making contact with the manager and creating a collaborative relationship. Simple information sheets outlining the program, its goals, and its importance to the students help to clarify the CBI process. The business shall receive tentative schedules, educational objectives, and introductions to the students and school staff.

Teachers can create an information sheet to elicit help from local businesses and to prepare them for the ongoing program. Once the initial groundwork is complete, time spent making contacts will be productive and consistent (see Appendix B11).

9. Teach and assess in the classroom, school, and community.

A large portion of the CBI process is devoted to the demonstration and guided practice of specific skills. The steps in this systematic process, created by a team of education professionals, does not diminish the importance of the teacher and student-teacher interaction. Teachers know standards, curriculum, assessment, and their students. They initiate the process, communicate with parents, facilitate IEP planning, and collaborate with all team members, but the primary duties of the teacher are planning, instruction, student practice, and student assessment. Therefore, all teachers must seek staff development in implementing standards and accountability systems, instructional methods of classroom management, behavior management, utilization of research, and the application of effective instruction.

Assessment must be as integrated into the entire CBI process as it is in all areas of instruction. Chapter 6 provides a complete discussion of assessment methods and interpretation. Collecting data about student performance is paramount to showing student achievement and instructional accountability. Matching standards, student outcomes, and curriculum are supported by evaluations. Therefore, thorough and ongoing assessment provides data for student evaluation, teacher effectiveness, and the value of CBI as an instructional method.

Teachers will find it is not necessary to complete all of the preliminary work, discussed up to this point, prior to entering the community. The amount of instruction in the community is totally dependent upon the students' needs. A community-referenced program for all students enhances parts of the curriculum not satisfied within the classroom. If the degree of needed support is substantial, much of the curriculum will be taught in the community, especially as students reach the later years of their program. Furthermore, whenever community instruction enters the curriculum, a few readiness items are essential. Early in the process teachers can instruct students on safety skills, including passenger safety, pedestrian safety, and appropriate behavior in various settings. Then, teachers should spend time on community awareness, such as knowing the types of businesses and locations in the local community. During this time, teachers make final connections with managers so all locations are ready for on-site instruction, which starts as soon as possible.

For students with support needs, possible formats for instruction in the community include either a spiral approach or a thematic approach. A spiral approach takes a broad scope initially, and then repeats instruction at the same locations with more skill acquisition. In the spiral approach, for example, elementary school classes begin with supervised pedestrian safety and then move on to such areas as community services, grocery stores, drug stores, and leisure activities. The overall emphasis in all of the locations would be appropriate behavior, awareness of the location, and simple layouts of sites. In the middle school classes, the same sequence would be followed—pedestrian safety, specific community services, grocery stores, drug stores, and leisure activities. The overall emphasis in all of the locations would be a review of behavior issues and layouts of sites, then continue to locating items, choosing sizes, prices, making payments, and increasing independence. Public transportation could be introduced in the middle school program. In the high school classes, the spiral approach encourages independent pedestrian safety. All locations would be revisited with an emphasis on making judgments about budgeting, consumer planning, and independent use of public transportation; living arrangements and employment sites would be added to the instructional program. In the spiral approach, each time a location is revisited, throughout the grade levels, more detail and increased independence is emphasized.

A thematic approach emphasizes units of study centered around specific skills and locations. For example, at the elementary grade level a unit on pedestrian safety and services within the school would be followed by work on community services available to the students, such as bike safety programs, personal identification programs, or the public library. In this respect, the middle school program teaches all skills needed in grocery stores, drug stores, and leisure activities. The high school concentrates on public transportation and community employment locations. Each theme includes knowledge of varied locations within the category, behavioral expectations, and total utilization of the services through the different sites.

The demographics of the district influence the appropriate type of approach. Currently, families are very mobile. Students move from neighborhood to neighborhood and in and out of the district. In some locations, teaching assignments change relatively often as well. In this situation, CBI is more comprehensive and more likely to expose each student to the same experiences using a spiral approach. Ongoing assessment may necessitate changing the overall classroom program from year to year, but each student would have their needs met and receive a complete program. On the other hand, if the district is in a community that has little movement within, or from outside, the thematic approach may be sequential and appropriate for the students. It would be consistent across levels and schools and easy to explain to the school board when asking for support. Whichever approach is used, the teaching and implementation in the community is crucial to the students' ability to generalize skills and gain independence needed for adult life. As mentioned earlier, the only drawback for students spending a large portion of the day in the community is their need to interact with their age peers and participate in the overall school program. The only restraint on this portion of the program is the fiscal situation of the district.

10. Evaluate the process based on student performance.

Program evaluation comes from three administrative levels: The classroom level, conducted by the teacher; the school level, conducted by the principal or supervisor; and the district level, conducted by a higher level administrator. This discussion addresses ongoing evaluation activities performed by the teacher and the program supervisor. Higher level evaluations consider the various disciplines of finances, public relations, curriculum and instruction, and personnel.

The reflective teacher is constantly judging if the instructional strategies being used are assisting students to meet standards and stated objectives. Teachers evaluate spontaneously during each lesson and in a more structured manner following each instructional unit. Teachers constantly ask themselves questions like: "Was the student able to perform the skill?" "Were my strategies effective?" "What was the best technique that I used?" "What should I change to make this lesson more productive?" Student performance is an excellent indicator of the methods' and materials' effectiveness. The teacher collects data not only on student performance, but also on the process and the teacher behavior that affected performance. Careful examination of the instructional methods and deliberate alterations made

Steps	Tasks to Complete
1. Communicate with students/parents.	• Notify parents of the interest inventory. • Ask for follow-up activities. • Help students prepare for school.
2. Conduct an ecological inventory.	• Get information about interests and preferences. • Get information about environments of choice. • Determine needs and goals.
3. Plan for individuals.	• Evaluate the general education curriculum. • Conduct transition meetings. • Develop units, lessons, and IEPs.
4. Acquire school support.	• Outline the benefits of using CBI. • Request permission. • Obtain financial support and transportation.
5. Develop curriculum.	• Revise the general education curriculum. • Determine needs of all students. • Develop scope, sequence, procedures, and supports.
6. Create a master plan.	• Consult the standards and assessment mandates. • Outline the instructional process systematically. • Write a flexible and comprehensive plan.
7. Plan instruction.	• Review class and individual goals. • Plan for content, presentations, and student activities. • Plan for assessment.
8. Research locations.	• Review the ecological inventory. • Consider focus and generalizability. • Make contacts and develop partnerships.
9. Teach and assess in the classroom, school, and community.	• Implement inquiry and direct instruction methods. • Provide for student practice. • Collect data, assess, and provide feedback.
10. Evaluate the process based on student performance.	• Consider all stakeholders. • Question the effectiveness of strategies used. • Make judgments based on results.

Figure 3.2   Implementing Community-Based Instruction Into the Curriculum

to each lesson reflect the information the teacher acquires about strategies, techniques, and student performance. In each case, the teacher must keep records that indicate student achievement. Minor changes and further evaluation of student performance becomes an ongoing, systematic process for the teacher. Self-evaluation continues from reflection about individual students to summative information gathered on the entire class over a term or year. Feedback from parents and administrators influences the teacher's account of the instructional effectiveness. With this information, the principal or supervisor will judge if the process is improving the acquisition of skills across the curriculum.

What Are Appropriate CBI Sites for Students Between Ages 18 and 21?

Typically students complete their high school program around age 18. IDEA `97 states that students with IEPs are entitled to remain in the school system until the end of the school year that they turn 21. Students with intermittent and limited support needs usually graduate with their class and continue on to the postsecondary plans they have designed. Students with extensive and pervasive support needs often choose to take advantage of the added years of service. Those final years present students with an excellent opportunity to literally move into the community, receive instruction in all areas of independent living, and make long-lasting connections with services they will need as adults.

Creative arrangements present a variety of opportunities. A perfect location, if available, is a classroom in a community college or 4-year university. The age of the individuals that attend college exactly matches the 18- to 21-year-old student with support needs. Another option, with the knowledge that the teacher must arrange as much interaction with same-age peers as possible, would be to place work oriented classes in businesses, corporations, or at work-sites. The modeling of other workers and the support of school staff could create valuable learning experiences. In other areas, classes emphasizing independent living might be set up in an apartment or a house in a neighborhood. In this setting, the total program is community-based and the strategies used to increase student independence require minimal generalization because they are in the actual location. The ideal program would have all of the above opportunities and students could choose a location or rotate locations throughout their last 3 years of school.

For the majority of classes that must remain within school buildings, students, families, and teachers need to make administrators aware of the need to conduct a large portion of the students' programs outside of the school building. This requires added financial support and transportation. Nevertheless, it is the final chance for students to make the smooth transition mandated in the IEP process. The instructional strategies do not change per se, however, the amount of time creating independence takes on a new focus. Early transition meetings should determine the age that the student and family plan to exit the system. That timeline should drive the program from the first transition meeting until the student's graduation and set in motion a plan that emphasizes Community-Based Instruction as its primary instructional strategy.

What Resources Are Needed to Support CBI?

Clearly, financial and curricular resources, as mentioned in the 10 steps above and in Figure 3.2, top the list of crucial factors. Nevertheless, human resources and corporate sponsorship also fulfill substantial needs. Parents nurture the use of CBI through the guidance they give their children. Administrators manage policy and legal factions. Within the student body and throughout the community, service organizations contribute time and facility support. Businesses and corporations donate training and materials. Without the contributions of people and facilities outside of school, the CBI program lacks natural settings that ensure student independence. Resources come from the following:

1. Parents

2. Administrators

3. Service organizations

4. Corporations

Of course, students may contribute some personal money to certain community activities and teachers sometimes contribute personal or classroom money to activities. The groups listed above, and described below, are the primary contributors of larger amounts of resources not possible on an individual or classroom basis.

Parents

Parents provide a large part of the human resources needed to implement a CBI strategy. A later discussion in this chapter describes how parents can support the use of CBI with follow-up activities at home, or by helping during the school day as a volunteer. As a resource, parents offer time, expertise, opportunities, and minor financial contributions. Parents may work on a large scale conducting fundraisers or individually providing an allowance to the student for their activities. In whatever capacity parents support the school program, they provide resources beyond what the school is able to furnish without their help.

Administrators

Administrative support, as mentioned earlier, is needed for permission to use CBI as an instructional strategy and allocating budget commitments to fund the total curriculum. Although budget, transportation, and insurance coverage represent the essential components of providing CBI as a curricular method, administrative support does not stop there. Staff development for teachers and paraprofessionals and extended planning time for making arrangements and choosing materials occurs through collaboration with administrators. Another area of administrative support is communication with families in initial stages, providing information on business connections and the school board. Grade level leaders, content area department heads, teachers, and team members can offer information to clarify major instructional issues for the administration. Fortunately, once procedures are established, administrators become efficient at attending to details of supporting Community-Based Instruction.

School and Community Service Organizations

Many high schools have incorporated service learning projects and volunteerism into their graduation requirements. School clubs may take on projects in which the students donate their time and talents for the betterment of others. Because all students benefit from community-referenced learning, a club's organizational support would have a large impact on the whole school. Community service organizations in large and small communities usually have specific programs that they support. For example, one of the missions of the Knights of Columbus is to support organizations that promote independence for individuals with extensive or pervasive support needs. Local Lions Clubs, Kiwanis, and Rotary Cubs are all service oriented and may contribute to a school program that they feel is essential to their community.

Corporations

Local businesses or major corporations may be approached to review their community education programs. Some corporations will concentrate on training for the purpose of employment with that company. Others will approach their outreach, education, and service projects as one entity and offer grants for those individuals or schools that satisfy a specified list of criteria. Larger corporations may have junior achievement projects, which involve middle or high school students in projects related to the product or service the corporation produces. A personal request from a teacher, parent, supervisor, or principal may reveal opportunities available to all students, that would support and enhance the school program.

What Support Systems Are Needed to Make CBI Successful?

Ongoing help from dedicated individuals leads to success in the community. Parents support the teacher's ability to conduct a comprehensive curriculum. The complicated job of assigning and training staff denotes administrative actions that promote sound procedures. The daily program functions through the work of the teachers, paraprofessionals, and related service personnel. Volunteers and peer helpers add individualization and sincere feedback to a greater number of students than the school could manage were they not involved. While most contributors maintain continual input, agency providers enter the picture near the end of the school year. They add a link that will carry the student into adulthood. Without any one of the above support systems, CBI strategies would be a set of related activities at best.

Parents

Parent input, permission, carryover of the process at home, and classroom involvement are the most important components of the community program. Parents provide support by demonstrating their interest in what their child is learning. While planning the individual transition and educational plans for the young adult with support needs, students and their parents express their desires. These desires will drive the overall program. As the teacher works with families to get a general idea about the major areas of instruction that are important, teachers will begin to develop a process that serves all students, some on an individual basis.

Granting formal permission for the student to participate in CBI is another form of parental support. Formal permissions slips, which meet the specifications of the district, are gathered before implementing the plans. The permission is necessary for liability purposes and will provide the information needed according to school district policy. Without parents' permission to travel off school grounds, the process is stalled and instruction that remains within the classroom is stifled by the limits of authenticity.

Parents can support the school program in many ways. They can encourage independence on the morning of an outing by reminding the student about the proper attire for the location. Parents can also inquire about the activities of a day and show sincere interest in the student's performance. Families reinforce skills learned in school by visiting similar locations on a family outing. Furthermore, assisting the class in the community or helping in the classroom is extremely supportive of the process. Parents who are involved with CBI implementation make a valuable contribution, but also learn how to continue the program at home. Both support the process and can further the learning abilities of all students.

Administrators

At this point, the school administration has been involved in many ways. They helped in the development stage, provided financial backing for CBI to occur, coordinated schedules, and assisted with inclusion efforts. The need for continued encouragement is ongoing, whether it is fostered in professional rhetoric about the process or by a description of the total school program through public promotion, staff development, or visitation. The daily need for administrative support may be minimal, but occasional follow-up and participation is helpful to the teachers and motivating for students.

Paraprofessionals

Paraprofessionals may be the only paid participants in the use of CBI besides the teacher. The duties of the paraprofessional are outlined first by their job description and next by the needs and responsibilities designated by the teacher. Their role is essential from several standpoints. First, they are employed by the district and would have the same liability backing as the teacher. Next, they have the safety, health, and procedural training to know the district rules and expectations. Paraprofessionals have day-to-day involvement with the students and know the overall goals for each student. The paraprofessional may manage students in the classroom while the teacher is in the community, or vice versa. It is not uncommon for a paraprofessional to be assigned to a specific student for a portion of the day to monitor behavior or progress in other areas. It is imperative that the paraprofessional has developed a rapport with the students and is in a position to give input and feedback on student progress and needs. Typically, the relationship between the teacher and the paraprofessional is one of respect and dependability. More than any other individual, the paraprofessional has significant influence on the success of using CBI as an instructional strategy.

Related Service Personnel

Most school programs are supported by speech therapists, physical and occupational therapists, vision and hearing specialists, and job coaches. These individuals have expertise in providing services to students that goes beyond the classroom teacher's training. Integrated therapy is a current best-practice that ensures that therapeutic activity is part of the daily routine. After consultation and demonstration, many times the teacher, paraprofessional, or volunteer can follow through with therapists' suggestions. Job coaches could make initial contacts and provide training to other individuals, including co-workers. This training provides a valuable service to both students and employees.

Volunteers

Volunteerism is gaining recognition as a viable service. The age or skill level of volunteers are unimportant when compared with their ability to communicate with students and follow the teacher's directions in the community. Volunteers may accompany an individual enroute to community sites, assist with duties on site, provide practice of skills in the classroom, and assist with documentation of student progress. A strong volunteer program may be coordinated at the district level, but should be relatively consistent with the specific class it supports. The training of a group of volunteers may be an administrative task; however, it is also worthwhile to consider hands-on training by direct participation with the use of CBI. Volunteers work for free. The acknowledgment, recognition, and gratitude offered to them will increase their enjoyment of the experience and emphasize the teachers' and school's appreciation.

Peer Helpers

What is more motivating than going shopping with a friend? Although CBI is much more systematic and intense than the typical social shopping trip, part of the goals are designed so that the student will gain enough independence to do just that. Peers must be informed of the importance of their involvement and the expectation that they will be learning supports, models, and behavioral examples for students who require their support. They are chosen by their interest, availability, maturity, and potential to increase the competencies of their peers. In most cases, the careful pairing of students can lead to increased learning for all involved. A consistent and productive plan for peer helpers can make a valuable contribution to the CBI process.

Service Learning

In addition to peer volunteers, schools across the country are implementing service learning programs for secondary students. Participating schools would require a given number of hours, spent providing an unpaid human service, for graduation. Teachers who have access to service learning programs can expand their in-school and community programs beyond what may be possible with volunteers and peer helpers. In schools where the service learning program requires a specific number of hours, students can be given responsible tasks to complete. The added dependability, and association with the school at large, has a unifying effect on the community program.

Agency Providers

Agencies cover a wide spectrum of services. Service agencies include mental health; advocacy agencies such as the ARC (formerly the Association for Retarded Citizens); supported employment, job partnership, and training agencies; disability specific agencies, such as The United Cerebral Palsy Association or the Association for Children with Learning Disabilities; therapeutic support services; and child health and welfare agencies. Agencies that are involved with students who require support should be involved in transition planning. There are several ways these agencies could help the CBI process. Some agencies provide equipment on loan and some provide training or job coaching. Other agencies will accompany an individual and encourage self-determination and self-advocacy. Local transition coordinating councils may appoint a primary agency, which works by a case-management approach, for accessing services. Collaboration of services among agencies can prevent a duplication of services and ensure that there will not be a lack of resources available to students. If secondary teachers participate with transition committees, they will have the knowledge of services for which the student may qualify. Agency involvement is also stressed in this chapter under partnerships.

How Are Support Systems Developed?

Deliberate efforts through letters, professional networking, and personal visits create the support systems described throughout this guide. Teachers, supervisors, parents, advocates, policymakers, and administrators develop working relationships with everyone they encounter. Sometimes a relationship initiated by professional contact leads to sharing common goals and challenges. The order used to develop support systems is neither sequential nor predictable. The best longterm constructive relationships evolve over years of participation in professional activities.

Contact Letters

Personal letters on school stationery to local proprietors, social organizations, and recreational facilities, followed by a scheduled visit are time efficient and considerate. Brochures stating the purpose of activities conducted in the community portion of the curriculum inform the non-education community about the total school program. Although CBI is a well-known practice in the special education discipline, it cannot be assumed that the general public knows or understands the far-reaching expectations of the process or how community members can cooperate with the instruction. Contact letters will bridge the gap until a personal contact is made.

Another source of support may come from individuals such as authors of articles, business corporate leaders, vendors, or individuals teachers meet in casual settings. The use of electronic mail and Internet searches have generated a large number of resources and individuals who may offer support. Written contact with these individuals may turn up some unexpected resources for the local school program or assist the teacher with planning and implementation of CBI activities.

Professional Contacts

Local and regional conferences are a good way to initiate professional contacts and learn about methods and techniques used outside of the teacher's school. A wealth of information is often shared, which will augment or confirm the instructional process being implemented in a district. Professional contacts share goals and challenges. Cooperative learning strategies expand to staff development activities, as well as those within the classroom. Most professionals are excited about what they have done to promote their programs and enjoy helping others who are in the process of developing their own strategies.

Personal Contacts

Personal contacts may be limited to friends, family members, local business facilities, or agencies, but are most likely to be the best source of support. A personal contact may follow a contact letter or be an initial phone call. In the case of employment locations, a phone message may be a much faster way to gain permission or cooperation than an unannounced visit. Scheduled appointments respect the time and job demands of personal contacts. Teachers should extend every courtesy when promoting the school program.

Networking

Expanding contacts beyond the classroom has no limits. Keeping a complete directory of acquaintances, professionals, business contacts, and agencies will allow individuals with similar goals to support each other. Networking is promoted wholeheartedly across affiliations. Teachers, parent groups, service agencies, and other professionals promote the positive aspects of sharing information among individuals with similar issues. Any participation in a network is optional and totally self-selected. Teachers who share needs and accomplishments are often welcomed into the networking process without obligation or commitment. The process is an excellent source of support and communication.

How Are Community Partnerships Developed?

Community partnerships occur with selective participation in organizations that embrace the same outcomes for students as the family and school. The word *selective* implies that teachers and administrators choose to spend time with agencies that promote student independence, community participation, and a long-term commitment to the success of all individuals. Some professional involvement will be in representative positions and some will be in leadership roles. The ultimate goal of a successful educational process includes the cohesiveness of community partners.

The Transition Task Force

If the district or region has created a transition task force, or coordinating council (dealing with students' movement to postschool activities), partnerships with agencies, business, and schools should be in place. Monthly meetings may be used to update young adults and their families on the latest legislation or introduce them to postschool options. Providers for adult living arrangements, mass transportation, and futures planning may also be represented or spotlighted at regularly scheduled meetings. Although employment is a primary focus of transition planning, mobility, transportation, independent living skills, and recreation are also components of the student-centered, outcome-based approach. All of these areas are emphasized through the school program, especially the coordination of services for students who require support.

Open Houses, Job Fairs, and Career Days

Activities sponsored by the school, vocational technical centers, or outside agencies are excellent opportunities to create partnerships. Working together to promote open houses, job fairs, career days, and interacting during planning and presentation stages all contribute to a better knowledge of the community. Any of these options would provide the chance to share information about the school's program, elicit technical or financial support, and obtain access to local training sites.

Mental Health and Mental Retardation Services

States and counties provide mental health and mental retardation services through local administrative units and offices. Individuals must be eligible for services by meeting criteria set by the agency, such as a disability or mental health diagnosis. In some states, a case-management system serves individuals. The case manager interviews the family and the individual, collaborates with school, attends all transition meetings, and helps with agency contacts. As the student leaves the school system, the case manager continues as the contact person for adult service programs. In other states, a managed care system provides a more global service by allocating a specific amount of per capita money to the locality. Individuals with disabilities access services based on the amount of fiscal support allotted to them. In either system, the federal, state, or local government provides financial support and regulations. The family initiates the partnership with the specific system and seeks help coordinating agency services.

Employment Agencies

Employment agencies focus on helping individuals acquire and maintain employment. These agencies may provide employment coaches and coordinators, others provide support with funding and summer jobs. The Office of Vocational Rehabilitation is a federal agency, which helps individuals with disabilities to obtain equipment to enable them to find competitive employment. If the individuals need intermittent or limited support, they can access the employment agencies geared at supporting the general public. Those with extensive support needs will require more direct intervention. In most cases, employment agencies get involved upon invitation near the end of the young adult's educational program. The agencies work on an eligibility basis and have a limited amount of services and funds available.

Partnerships with employment agencies result from school contacts who learn of the agency, what is available, and how to access the service. A transition coordinating committee should include representatives from the most prominent agencies within the community. The more schools and agencies work together, the better they understand the goals and responsibilities of each other. Striving for good participation increases opportunities for students.

Service Organizations

Partnerships with local organizations are limited only by the availability of those organizations in the community and contacts that creative and diligent teachers, parents, and school officials make outside of school. Service organizations may offer financial support or provide human resources. They can help with connections that lead directly or indirectly to employment, volunteers to assist with direct programming, and periodical support for specific requests. Depending on the organization's mission and member expertise, long-term, mutual partnerships can transpire that benefit the organization and all students.

Conclusion

The development of CBI is a dynamic process. Instruction is constantly changing as students demonstrate their need for instruction in the community. A systematic, sequential process and the involvement of the stakeholders allows for consistency and flexibility of instruction. Recognizing and addressing challenges early in the process set the stage for success. The wise use of human and fiscal resources creates a base to establish a progressive, multilevel system that is well organized and has continuity. Effective classroom strategies and the use of natural environments prepare students to function in the community with increased independence. Finally, support systems and partnerships allow the community to be involved in the education of its future citizens. No effective intervention can exist without total involvement of all concerned.

Case Study 3.1

Kathy Jones, a secondary special education teacher assigned to a program for students with extensive support needs, was asked to participate in developing a general curriculum guide to support her students. After 2 weeks of feeling overwhelmed, she contacted her program supervisor. The supervisor quickly eased Kathy's tensions by emphasizing that the curriculum development would be accomplished over the summer by a team of individuals. Kathy felt much better when she realized she was not alone in the endeavor.

Over a 2-month period, each member of the team collected information to bring to the committee. Bill, the general educator, collected the district curriculum and standards and highlighted all items that seemed essential to independent adult life. Mark, the school psychologist collected assessment tools and vocational items. Julie, the program master teacher, worked on coordinating schedules, work locations, and inviting parent and community representatives to serve on the committee. Kathy compiled a list of common IEP goals that were consistently repeated for her students over the last 4 years.

At the end of the school year, the team planned 3 structured weeks to outline a curriculum for the high school general education program. With the help of the school secretary, the team constructed a first draft of a comprehensive curriculum. The plan was that five teachers would use the curriculum over the next school year. They would meet twice during the year to discuss the integration of activities, effective forms of assessment, and progress toward implementation.

Kathy was exhausted but thrilled with the document the team had started. She had no idea that so much effort went into curricular planning or that it was such a dynamic process. The curriculum evolved over the next 2 years. It never seemed completely finished, but the guide was comprehensive, flexible, and usable. All students were able to participate in community activities, as needed, to meet the state standards. Students receiving support from Kathy for daily living standards consistently received their instruction and assessment outside of their usual classroom.

Forms Related to Chapter 3—Appendix B

Appendix B1   Pre-Inventory Notice

Appendix B2   Newsletter Article

Appendix B3   Parent Handbook Page

Appendix B4   Permission Slip

Appendix B5   Sample Ecological Inventory

Appendix B6   District Permission Form

Appendix B7   Requesting Support

Appendix B8   General Lesson Plan Format

Appendix B9   Sample Lesson Plan

Appendix B10   Transition Site Survey

Appendix B11   Initial Meeting, Follow-Up Contract

Points to Ponder

1. How would you as a teacher approach challenges that are beyond your level of responsibility in order to reduce the barriers to CBI?

2. How can the local school district determine who needs to participate in CBI activities—since the CBI instructional strategy is a dynamic process—outside the classroom and how will those activities be developed?

3. How can the individual school or teacher acquire the resources to support the use of CBI?

4. How can the various stakeholders in CBI work together to implement effective strategies?

5. What strategies would be helpful in determining the best locations in the community to conduct instruction?

Suggested Reading

Brolin, D.E. (1997). *Life centered career education: A competency based approach* (5th ed.). Arlington, VA: The Council for Exceptional Children.

Edgar, E., & Polloway, E.A. (1994). Education for adolescents with disabilities: Curriculum and placement issues. *Journal of Special Education, 27*, 438-453.

Lyon, S.R., Domaracki, G.A., & Warsinske, S.G. (1990). *Community membership. Preparation for integrated community living and employment: Curriculum and program development.* Harrisburg, PA: Pennsylvania Department of Education.

Ryndak, L.L., & Alper, S. (1996). *Curriculum content for students with moderate and severe disabilities in inclusive settings.* Boston: Allyn & Bacon.

Sitlington, P.L., Clark, G.M., & Kolstoe, O.P. (2000). *Transition education and services for adolescents with disabilities.* Boston: Allyn & Bacon.

Westling, D.L., & Fox, L. (2000). *Teaching students with severe disabilities* (2nd ed.) Upper Saddle River, NJ: Merrill/Prentice Hall.

Chapter 4

Community-Based Instruction in the Curriculum: School and Classroom Component

In this chapter . . .

◆ What community and citizenship skills are needed by all students?

◆ How does the general curriculum address functional community skills?

◆ When should the teacher consider alternative curriculum approaches?

◆ What are the functional skills all students need?

◆ What are appropriate outcomes for the transition portion of the IEP?

◆ What are the goals and objectives for IEPs?

◆ What community-related skills and activities can be taught throughout the school?

What Community and Citizenship Skills Are Needed by All Students?

Today, the school reform movement, including the establishment of high standards and accountability, has made the curriculum cover a broad spectrum of academics. Everything covered in school is related to adult life in the greater community to some extent. Subject area specialists can explain how content relates to long-term proficiency as an adult in society. This discussion is general in nature; therefore, the broad topics of postsecondary training, employment, and general independent living are combined into the concept of students entering society as productive citizens. Every adult recognizes the need for economic knowledge, attention to health and safety issues, income and benefit needs, and the value of contributing to the community by caring for the overall needs of all citizens. In this sense, these skills represent the primary community and citizenship content that must be addressed within the curriculum.

As subject area experts responded to reform issues, several generalities emerged that lead to curriculum changes, which were designed to prepare students for the world they face upon graduation. Key areas of emphasis include coverage of content, not mere facts, problem-solving through critical and creative thought processes, integration across subject areas, standards for all students, and cooperative abilities needed to solve problems and complete group goals (Pugach & Warger, 1996). These collective goal areas directly relate to community skills needed by all citizens. The best environment for instruction may be the actual ecological setting where the skill is used. For example, on election day, when there is a voting poll in every precinct, all students can benefit from seeing the voting process first hand. Or, students could attend a school board meeting at which budget issues or curriculum are discussed. Clearly, common, everyday examples such as these can be directly addressed within the basic curriculum.

The general curriculum is driven by standards in subject area content. Pugach and Warger (1996) offered a comprehensive overview of curricular trends and how they relate to skills needed by all students. The following is a brief discussion of some global subject-related concepts. To relate the community and citizenship needs of all students to curriculum trends, a concentrated study in each subject area would be warranted. This glimpse of current trends takes examples from the content in science, math, and social studies. General concepts are depicted in the following information:

1. Scientists recognize the importance of understanding the way science is practiced. They realize that the highest level of motivation comes from the study of items that are experiential in nature. Important content includes the interaction of systems such as the solar system and weather, general patterns of change, and the cycles of interrelated systems.

2. Math is seen as a way to deal with quantities, spatial arrangement, and the interpretation of data. Math must address the real needs of jobs and living through systematic thought, not symbol manipulation.

3. Experts have often questioned the role of social studies in the curriculum. More than any other subject, social studies has been taught in themes that are presented at specific grade levels. Part of the reason for some of the controversy has been the debate over a definition of social studies. Most definitions come back to the concept of citizenship training. The concern then becomes, what kind of citizenship training should be emphasized? Do schools promote citizens in the light of a patriot, a survivor, a reformer, or a policymaker?

These examples display concepts that help students function in and out of school. A scope and sequence can be loosely devised for all subjects. Assessment determines what a student has mastered and when a student needs more instruction. The relevance of the instruction and the appropriate setting has long been the professional academic judgment of the teacher with the support of administrators. It is clear that the school and community offer many variables that can be included in curricula areas.

How Should the General Curriculum Address Functional Community Skills?

As students choose their course of study prior to entering high school, their curriculum becomes a combination of basic skills and specialized content needed for their next environment. That environment can be a college classroom or a vocational setting. The critical question is, "What is functional in that community?" If the word *functional* indicates relevant, meaningful content, teachers can begin to conceptualize functional skills in all areas of the curriculum. Taken literally, the community skills then become the skills needed for relevant participation in and out of the classroom and the practice of skills that lead to independent adult behavior.

The activities below show how the general curriculum can address functional community skills. States set the standard, the districts derive the curriculum from the standards, and the teacher uses activities to teach the curriculum content. The intensity of the activities in meeting the needs of students is totally dependent on the students' level of performance, their need for support, and resources the teacher has available.

1. In the college environment, students need independent study skills. Reference skills are taught in the classroom and in collaboration with the school librarian. After students receive instruction in this supportive environment, they can be asked to locate information in the public library.

2. Students can learn to give and receive directions as they would on a work-site to demonstrate site-specific skills. Asking for help and applying the language of the trade both lead to success in that vocation. Teachers can provide activities to let students practice all of these skills in the classroom and in school settings. At some time in the school year, skills transfer from the comfort of school to the authenticity of the work-site.

3. Role-play a sequence to solve this dilemma: While waiting in line at the drug store, a student places his keys on the magazine rack. He did not notice the keys were missing until he went to put his coat in his locker. What should he do?

The general education curriculum must add relevance and meaning to learning in order for students to willingly and wholeheartedly participate. Much of instruction is activity-based. The activities used to present the content of the curriculum can be used to address functional community skills.

When Should the Teacher Consider Alternative Curriculum Approaches?

The Individuals with Disabilities Education Act of 1997 (IDEA '97) mandated access to the general curriculum for all students. This focus indicated that the instructional needs of students with disabilities be addressed through the general curriculum. In most cases, the general curriculum is taught through teachers using specific methods. As Pugach and Warger (1996) pointed out, students need to benefit from the method. To be able to do that, they must have the concentration, social skills, and communication to access the method's process and content. Therefore, access is not just a right of exposure to content, but the ability to benefit from the process used to present the content. Thus, the challenge is much more involved than simply a matter of access or exposure to curricula.

With this view of access in mind, schools recognize that students with extensive or pervasive support needs may require unique methods of instruction outside of the general classroom. Most often, these approaches include time spent in a classroom where an adapted or alternative curriculum is presented using specialized instruction individualized for the student. The students in this example may participate in alternative state assessments geared directly at their individual goals and programs of instruction. These students may demonstrate increased success when their classroom program is paired with a graduated amount of time spent directly in community locations.

When alternative placements are considered, students may spend a small portion or the majority of the school day in a community location, depending upon the physical or medical needs of the student. Most districts place the support classroom within grade level areas in elementary, middle, and high schools. Students have access to all curriculum subjects, special subjects such as music, and nonacademic activities. Classroom time is spent meeting IEP goals and working on skills generalization. Much of the school day is spent between this class and the age-appropriate grade. When students have difficulty transferring skills, instruction goes to the exact locations, or ecological settings, to reduce the need for broad generalization of acquired skills. Much of what follows in this chapter and Chapter 5 supports direct instruction for students with extensive support needs.

What Are the Functional Skills All Students Need?

Thorough student assessment, student and family desires, and long-term goals for the future determine the skills needed by each student. Formal and informal inquiries clarify the student's current levels of performance and individual needs. Competency lists such as those in Appendix A, based on the *Life Centered Career Education* (*LCCE;* Brolin, 1997) curriculum and the modified version of the *LCCE*, give an overview of the skills students with extensive support needs must have to function independently. Educators agree that students with support needs require appropriate instruction that will prepare them to function in their communities. The collection listed below reflects a basis for planning instruction, which will occur throughout the school, in the classroom, and, later, in the community. The remainder of this chapter emphasizes school and classroom instruction and includes several "how-to" activities:

1. Applied academic skills.

2. Employment and vocational skills.

3. Independent living skills: shopping and home living.

4. Social skills: Interpersonal skills, hygiene and grooming, personal management.

5. Leisure and recreation skills.

...priate Outcomes for the Transition Portion of the IEP?

...es drive the IEP goals for students receiving special services in secondary ...ired by IDEA '97, the IEP team must state planned courses at age 14 and ...outcomes by age 16. Discussions about what students desire for their future ...e family has made for their young adult family members can be incorporated ...ion section of the IEP. Before the IEP team meets to discuss transition out-...s should gather results from aptitude tests and vocational assessments, contact ...ies that will support the student as an adult, and organize enough information ...ductive meeting. The transition plan and IEP goals (including the CBI program) ...tively create experiences needed to achieve transition outcomes.

...ndary Training

...ndary training should be designed to promote formal instruction once high school is ...te. The most effective postsecondary training prepares the student for productive ...yment. Some examples of postsecondary training include apprenticeships, trade schools, ...d services, adult career and technical training programs, continuing education programs, ...ness schools, community colleges, and universities. These options cover a wide range of ...ining opportunities commensurate with student abilities. For instance, Bill has specific learn-...g disabilities in reading and sustaining attention. He has a desire to be a social worker, for ...hich he needs a college degree. Bill may attend a community college that will enable him to ...learn how to adjust to the demands and freedoms of college. In addition, he will acquire the academic support he needs to succeed. The community college will help Bill get accepted at a 4-year college to complete his degree. Likewise, Jan likes to cook and has extensive support needs. She is an accurate, steady worker and is neat and clean. A tourist resort near her home has a 2-year training program for prospective cooks, housekeepers, and lawncare workers. During her senior year, at age 20, Jan enrolled in the program, which continued for 1 year after graduation. Both are examples of postsecondary training.

School performs many functions in developing postsecondary outcomes. The larger responsibilities involve coordinating of families and career counselors to determine students' interests and preferences, researching postsecondary options, and understanding what knowledge and skills are needed to be accepted in the postsecondary setting. Consider the two students discussed above. In Bill's situation, he must take required high school courses needed for college acceptance as well as entrance exams. It is important that Bill understand his needs and be able to disclose information (self-advocacy) that will help him acquire the support he requires for success in the postsecondary environment. For Jan, the school may help by taking responsibility for obtaining uniforms and workbooks and providing a liaison with the business or school. Jan's time spent in school will concentrate on reinforcing the basic skills needed for her job.

The activities in the curriculum that support postsecondary outcomes incorporate exploring options and taking required courses. Once decisions are made, teachers can assist students in making contacts with their chosen training site and determining requirements of

Applied Academic Skills

The mastery of academic skills should be a high priority of schooling. The public considers all other activities, such as sports and social events, as extracurricular. For students with limited support needs in inclusionary settings, academic subjects that regular education students take must be available for all students. Teachers can continually reinforce the need to concentrate on practical, frequently needed academics for students who have postsecondary goals that do not include college.

When teaching students with extensive or pervasive support needs, educators must emphasize the type of academic content needed to demonstrate independence. In this case, applied academic skills enable students to demonstrate behaviors that help them to take the isolated, functional content taught in the classroom and use it appropriately to gain products and services within the community. Teachers should forego an overabundance of reading, creative writing, and advanced math concepts in favor of basic computation and deliberate reading for information. In this respect, the elementary and early middle school programs provide intensive academic instruction, and the later middle school and high school programs focus on community skills.

Employment and Vocational Skills

Students should have work goals throughout their educational experience. The *LCCE* outlines work-related goals for each school level. In elementary school, students should take part in career awareness activities. In middle school, students should engage in career exploration experiences. In high school, students should concentrate on career preparation activities. Work-related skills, such as cooperation, task completion, time and money management, high standards of quality, and the acceptance of supervision, should be emphasized throughout the levels. For older students, the transition plan and IEP outline how specific vocational skills and behaviors will be taught. A student's ultimate employment goal should be real, on-the-job work, because students who practice skills in settings other than a workplace receive only simulated practice. Work provides a gateway to independence. Therefore, all tasks taught through the CBI program should transfer to gainful, competitive employment.

Independent Living Skills: Shopping, Home Living

When using the term *independent living skills or life skills*, educators refer to a set of activities that allow an individual to be self-sufficient in all areas required for adult life. This broad term encompasses many subareas. Psychologists use the term *adaptive living skills* to refer to how an individual adjusts to the dynamic environments in which they function. Regardless of the terminology, the public judges students by their ability to blend into their surroundings without undue attention or extensive assistance. Curriculum must include all of the activities that make independent living outcomes a reality.

An example of independent living skills can be seen by looking at how Kevin, a 20-year-old man with extensive support needs, travels to visit his grandmother in a neighboring town. Kevin lives with his mother, who works in the public library on Saturdays. Each

Saturday, Kevin gets up at 9:00 AM; makes himself cereal, toast, and juice for breakfast; washes his face, brushes his teeth and shaves; puts on jeans, a clean T-shirt, socks, shoes, a jacket, and a baseball cap. At 10:00 AM, Kevin leaves the house, locks the door, and walks three blocks to a bus stop. He gets on bus number 4 at 10:20 AM. Kevin rides the bus about 20 minutes until it stops in front of the post office in the next town. Kevin walks around the post office to the parking lot where his grandmother is waiting. Kevin learned these skills through the collaborative effort of school, his extended family, and the public transit system.

Grocery shopping also demands a high priority when learning independent living skills. Shopping for all of life's needs and desires is a weekly activity for most adults. The skills learned in grocery shopping transfer to shopping of any kind, such as drug store shopping or leisure shopping at a mall. Despite the complexity of grocery shopping, the supermarket provides an environment rich with natural reinforcers, such as common products, space, and people. A grocery store displays an abundance of age-appropriate motivators like magazines and snacks. Therefore, before students go to the store, teachers need to reinforce advance planning, creating a list, locating items, paying for the items, and proper storage of purchases.

As part of the independent living curriculum, instruction for skills needed to function at home is essential. Although these skills can be taught at home, there are many opportunities to practice and utilize home living skills in school. Students can take cooking classes and have cleaning experiences of many kinds. Skills should include home safety, community services, and leisure activities that can be integrated into the daily school routine. Teachers can search for locations within the school that require home living skills. Perhaps school personnel responsible for specific housekeeping duties would allow a student to shadow them or perform part of the task with them, such as preparing food in the cafeteria or cleaning the lobby or student lounge. Finally, parents can help by making the student responsible for a portion of routine homemaking duties at home.

Social Skills: Interpersonal Skills, Hygiene and Grooming, Personal Management

Interpersonal skills should be included in each subject area in the curriculum and in every instructional unit. Students need to learn to read social situations and respond appropriately. Interpersonal skills begin at birth, but special education programming delivers direct instruction to the students about interacting with others and cooperating in social situations. Much emphasis must be put on the communication aspect of social skills. Use role-playing to practice recognizing appropriate behavior in the community and responding to people students encounter. Leisure and social activities require less formal behavior, yet a specific set of social skills, just the same. Social settings provide a wide variety of situations for interpersonal interaction.

Direct instruction at home and school teaches a young adult to perform hygiene skills independently. For example, one teacher bought 12 plastic baskets at a discount store. With a small PTA stipend, she bought two hair dryers, an electric razor for each boy, and lip gloss and hair items for each girl. She asked local drug companies to supply shampoo, toothbrushes, toothpaste, and deodorant for each student. These were kept in the basket. Every morn-

ing a peer came into the classroom and helped
Grooming suggestions were implemented during the
break, the baskets were sent home and students were
ance and complete the tasks at home. Another teacher
fill a shave kit or cosmetic bag for his or her adolescent. Th
manner.

Good hygiene increases acceptance in work and social settings
self-concept. When directing students in hygiene matters, teache
explicit. They need to be careful not to make comments that will
or their primary caretaker. How something is said often overshad
instance, if a student needs to use deodorant, a teacher could say,
teenagers, our body changes and there are things we need to begin to
adults use deodorant every day. Deodorant is provided in our supplies."
sonal pronouns and making generalized, yet direct comments, the point
students with pervasive support needs approach secondary school, hygiene
Teachers can create a checklist for school and home for the students to fo
time of day and hygiene actions that are to be taken. Typically, by age 5, pa
tors, and peers look for a child to manage most of their own basic personal
Therefore, if hygiene issues persist into high school, they must be addressed pro
Appendix C2).

Personal management goes well beyond communication to include behavior, self-c
and social problem-solving. Students should have opportunities to participate in a wide
ety of situations that will expose them to different behavioral requirements. They sho
have the chance to think through problems, such as when to talk to peers, what to ta
about, and how to seek assistance. Teachers have partial control of the environment whe
they select locations for instruction. Teachers have no control over other people who will be
at a location or how they will act. The time immediately after a situation, or, at the latest,
the time back in the classroom, is the best time to debrief students on the situation, how
they responded, and the effectiveness of that action. If necessary, students can role-play possible alternative or replacement behaviors.

Leisure and Recreation Skills

Train students how to choose available and affordable ways to spend their free time. Unfortunately, students with extensive or pervasive support needs often have more free time than the typical teenager. Lack of employment, transportation challenges, and safety concerns often inhibit these young adults from total participation in activities. School offers an opportunity for students to participate in activities beyond what a family can usually provide. Schools have cultural performances, sporting events, and social activities. Students can visit local recreation areas and participate in organized activities. Teachers can offer strategies to help students identify their interests in a variety of activities and teach them how to independently arrange their participation in those activities. Families can help their young adults with ways to interact with others and enjoy leisure settings (see Appendix C1).

admission to that location. Interviews with peers who have chosen similar options can be helpful. Peers can explain procedures and expectations from their perspectives. Students with disabilities may need ongoing academic support to maintain entry-level ability or may require practice training in the areas they seek after graduation. Strategies stated in the IEP must be directly related to supporting the student in the ultimate postsecondary outcome.

Employment

Students must pursue optimistic and realistic employment outcomes, while seeing employment options as a continuum.

Competitive employment describes the type of paid work that provides economic and psychological satisfaction to the individual. Most adults expect to spend much of their day at work earning a living. Many students will need supported employment services. Supported employment involves real work, integrated settings, competitive pay, and ongoing support from a job coach or another employee. Other employment options include work crews, training facilities, and sheltered workshop programs. Use these options only when the student needs pervasive support while preparing for other options. Work preparation should be part of the transition plan for students with any level of support needs.

Stepping Stones		Reasonable Prerequisite		Ultimate Goal
Supervised Work Crews	➜	Supported Employment	➜	Competitive Employment

A large portion of any curriculum focuses directly or indirectly on work-related skills. Activities that promote competitive employment include locating and investigating worksites, ensuring that the student has the ability to travel to and from work independently, and managing money in a manner that will lead to self-sufficiency. Considering employment outcomes prior to postsecondary training and independent living needs helps clarify productive ways to meet the goals and objectives of all outcome areas. The IEP team should not find it difficult to locate the necessary training in the general curriculum and include those skills as IEP goals. Therefore, comprehensive outcomes are more important than the exact categories used to specify the transition plan outcomes.

Independent Living

Transition outcomes in the area of independent living include where students will live after graduation, how they will participate in the community, and how they will spend their free time. The IEP team seeks residential environments that range from total independence to supervised living to family living arrangements. The IEP team should link students with living arrangement providers as part of the transition plan. The activities needed to function independently, such as shopping, maintaining a schedule, and using private or public transportation, take many years to master.

Mandates also require that outcomes projecting leisure and recreational activities be included in transition plans. Young adults need leisure time activities to maintain a happy and healthy adult life. Self-advocacy skills play an important part in helping young adults articulate their preferences in leisure areas and gain the community support that they need for total participation. The preparation to function in residential and leisure areas are an important part of instruction.

It is extremely important that the IEP team that designs the transition plan includes the student in the process. Transition outcomes must be based on the student's needs and desires. Too often, teams fall into the trap of listing options that are readily available and overlook extended possibilities. Finally, transition coordinators need to know the regulations and expectations of their state and district prior to writing transition plans. A clear understanding of family desires, state standards, and school resources make the transition planning process productive and clarify how the use of CBI will support specially designed instructional needs.

What Are the Goals and Objectives for IEPs?

Goals and objectives for those items that require specially designed instruction should be listed in the IEP. The IEP team determines goal areas for students based upon their individual needs. Students can receive special services in any number of locations. The regular education classroom represents one location, and the local community is another. Goal areas in the IEP for individuals with disabilities at the secondary level may include the following:

1. Academic skills

2. Communication skills

3. Social skills

4. Vocational skills

5. Health skills

6. Independent living skills

7. Leisure skills

8. Self-determination skills

The IEP team bases the goals, written in the IEP upon the present levels of performance of each student and uses the format and specificity that complies with state and district guidelines. The team develops goals and benchmarks that may be used to support the transition plan using CBI as a method. The discussion below provides a brief example of items that may be included under each goal heading.

Academic Skills

Reading	Sight words, safety words, simple directions, newspaper ads, pleasure reading, such as comics or magazines
Math	Computation—addition, subtraction, multiplication, division, problem-solving, estimation, tax, tipping, calculator use, telling and estimating time, handling money
Content areas	Vocabulary, basic concepts, functional content, maps, directions, environmental issues, health and safety

Communication Skills

Verbal communication	Speaking clearly, answering questions, topic maintenance, rules of discourse, use of nonverbal communication devices
Basic writing skills	Personal information, simple notes, lists, letters, content area responses, use of word processing

Social Skills

Interaction with others	Peers, school officials, community members
Self-regulation	Appropriate behavior for specific settings

Vocational Skills

Work-related skills	Attendance, punctuality, initiative, following directions, working with co-workers, accepting supervision
Task-related skills	Dexterity, strength, specific job skills

Health Skills

Personal hygiene	Cleanliness, hair care, proper clothing
Proper diet	Food selection, balance, safe food handling
Fitness	Exercise, emotional stability
Routine medical attention	Doctor, dentist, eye care, specialty care
Safety issues	Pedestrian safety, home safety, stranger safety

Independent Living Skills

Shopping	Grocery store, drug store, department store
Cooking	Food planning, storage, preparation, clean-up
Home care	Cleaning, lawn care, safety
Community participation	Restaurants, services
Residential selection	Exploring options, judging options

Leisure Skills

Selecting options	Available, enjoyable, safe, affordable
Making arrangements	Inquiries, reservations
Participation	Joining a group, contributing to a group

Self-Determination Skills

Making informed choices and decisions	Following a systematic process
Seeking support	Asking for help when necessary

(See Appendixes C2 and C3)

What Community-Related Skills and Activities Can Be Taught Throughout the School?

The classroom represents the most common location for instruction. Without a doubt, the community offers the most natural setting for instruction, practice, and evaluation to occur. Nevertheless, it is unrealistic to expect that all instruction can occur on site. Teachers can still use real materials, authentic experiences, and activities that provide drill and practice within the confines of the classroom or school building. This discussion gives several examples of how the school or classroom may be used as a training site. The two examples below incorporate activities that can be used with a wide range of ages and abilities. "Real Practice School Activities" can be used throughout the school to practice community skills. Students in late elementary school and middle school, students with limited support needs, and students who receive all of their instruction in regular education may have little time in their schedules to participate in on site activities. Activities completed on school property provide added practice in independent skills.

Younger students, or students with extensive support needs, can benefit from classroom shopping activities using role-playing with authentic materials. The section titled "Management" outlines a possible way to tie behavior and budgeting into the shopping scenario. The concept of "Community-in-a-Box" captures the necessity of creating a community and making it manageable within a classroom. The activity supports the tremendous need that teachers have to ensure their materials are durable, long lasting, and well organized. This concept also incorporates a behavior program that provides incentives (pay) that may be used to make purchases. All academic, social, and performance tasks should be taught in the classroom. It works well to tie the budget and behavior systems in with the shopping units to allow for money, real or simulated, to make purchases. The following offers samples of instructional activities in the classroom.

Real-Practice School Activities

1. School cafeteria, student lounge, snack area

2. School store

3. Assemblies

4. Appointments

5. After-school, on-premises events

1. School cafeteria, student lounge, snack area

Shopping practice may occur in any school area that requires the use of money. To be sensitive to the students' ability level, make initial visits during low-traffic hours. Practice walking through the cafeteria line prior to the first lunch period. Cafeteria workers should also be involved in the training. If untrained individuals watch teachers model the language, procedures, and possible student reactions, they are likely to carry through with the process during high-traffic times. The same process can occur in student lounges or snack areas. During class time there will be few peers using the facility. As part of the instruction, practice determining price, judging if the student has enough money, and what kind of change to expect. Begin with a simple purchase and progress to more than one item. It will be up to the student when they use the facility alone to decide if they want the item chosen during practice, or if they would like to choose another selection. Students are responsible for their own money when making purchases. At lunch, use lunch money sent from home. In the case of free lunch benefits, make arrangements to purchase a small item when money is available from special projects.

2. School store

The school store usually sells school-pride items. Students will need permission and money from their parents to purchase items. A letter encouraging the parents to provide a small allowance for the items is one way to begin to teach the value of saving for desired items. Often, school stores are managed by a class or service club. This makes it especially important that students are able to make their purchases independently. An excellent project would be for different classes to run the store and provide sales practice as well. This gives the students tremendous practice with small or single item purchases, making change, and practicing work-related behaviors.

3. Assemblies

Most schools present a few assemblies to the student body each year. The programs consist of safety presentations, musical productions, or high-interest activities. Schools sponsor assemblies; therefore, money is not an issue. These occasions allow students to practice manners, self-regulated behavior, attention, and appropriate social interaction. Students get the opportunity to function within a very large group, follow directions, and observe behavioral standards. Again, practice going into the auditorium when it is empty to give students added confidence when they face the confusion of a large crowd.

4. Appointments

Everyday life includes numerous appointments. Parents might ask when appointments are needed in school. Think about times when students are expected to be at a certain place at a given time, such as athletic physicals, guidance counseling sessions, driver training, IEP meetings, recruiting interviews, and tutoring sessions. Actually, there are numerous opportunities to maintain a schedule. Providing students with a daily planner, making sure they wear a watch, instructing students about how to estimate the time needed to get to the location, and reinforcing the possibility that the other party may not be ready when they arrive all present crucial life skills that can easily be taught within the school.

5. After-school, on-premises events

All school levels sponsor after-school events. Elementary schools have extended programs and clubs, middle schools have clubs and sports, and high schools have sports, clubs, and practice for performances. Whether the students are participants or spectators, these activities offer enjoyable, age-appropriate leisure time. Faculty and staff supervise the programs and monitor safety issues. The activities supply physical and social opportunities in a relatively stress-free atmosphere. These events should not be used as instructional sessions. However, using instructional time to prepare for the activity can be beneficial. Discussing use of equipment, appropriate behavior, and ways to increase social interaction will build necessary skills for students to enjoy full participation.

Classroom activities

Most students typically spend the majority of their day in the classroom, despite the push to be in the community as much as possible. In late elementary or early middle school, teachers spend a portion of their instructional time preparing students for community participation and employment. When using simulation, activities should resemble the natural settings as closely as possible. In some cases, the activity can be integrated into behavior programs, independent living skills, or activities that combine academics and routine events. Intertwine leisure activities throughout classroom activities so students learn the expectations of behavioral and procedural concepts before they enter the community.

The following section describes activities that may be used in the classroom during those times when students need to practice prerequisite skills or when instruction in the community is not feasible. The management activities combine a token behavior system in which the token economy is based on traditional banking skills. The section titled "Community in a Box" utilizes shopping and recreational skills in activities that can be done in the typical classroom space. Both sections are easily adaptable to a variety of topics or skill levels.

Management

Management	Community in a Box
1. Behavior	1. Snack shop—snacks, fast food
2. Banking	2. Mini-mart—shopping
3. Budget	3. Gift shop-rewards
	4. Post office
	5. Town theater

Behavior: The most successful behavior plans teach students self-discipline and provide for a positive learning environment. This system ties into the banking and shopping programs described below. The teacher posts the rules, makes sure the students understand the meaning, and discusses the rules frequently in order to provide reinforcement. Students earn rewards as "money" or as certificates. Every hour the student can earn up to four points based on their compliance with the rules. At the end of the day, students exchange points for "money," which they put into "savings." Students may receive bonuses for exceptional behavior or certificates such as "One Free Soda" or "WOW, What an Improvement." Teachers can charge students for rule infractions or lack of attention to responsibility. The student must pay the nominal fees from their savings accounts in the way adults pay for parking tickets (see Appendix C4).

Banking: As described above, a teacher may generate "money" through the use of the behavior system. Students may also earn money as paychecks in conjunction with a classroom employment system. A system like this requires the students to deposit money into a savings account daily. One day a week, students may make a withdrawal.

Budget: Students with minimal reading skills can use a picture and envelope budget system. Label envelopes with pictures according to predetermined categories, such as "Savings account," "Snack shop," "Mini-mart," "Gift shop," "Post office," and "Town theater." As students earn "money" they make a deposit into their savings accounts. Later, the students utilize the money in the envelopes to finance their "trip" to that location. Prior to visiting a location, students remove their money from the envelope and put it into their wallets. If they have difficulty managing their wallets or overspend in one location, students may take their envelope with them (see Appendixes C5, C6).

Snack Shop	
Purpose:	To practice restaurant skills
Skills:	*Academic*: reading menus, survival reading, money skills, following written directions *Communication*: clearly indicate selection *Social*: using manners, pleasant conversation
Materials:	Tables, tablecloths, food from cooking classes, paper plates, silverware, cups, soda/drink, serving utensils, trays, napkins, cash register, calculator, money, store signs—"Place order here" and "Pick up order here"—order board, order selections, pencil, aprons, name tags, wallet, and tip card

Set Up for Fast Food Method:	1. Bring snacks from cooking class.
	2. Set up food table.
	   a. food cut in servings and put on plates
	   b. silverware
	   c. drinks already poured
	   d. trays for orders
	   e. signs
	3. Set up a table or desk for cashier.
	   a. cash register
	   b. coins for change
	   c. pencils and order blanks with selections
	   d. order board with "This Week's Selections" sign
	   e. sign—"Place Order Here"
	4. Wear aprons.
	5. Put tablecloths on the tables.
	6. Teacher and assistant help the cashier and the food worker.

Directions:	1. Students who are the patrons get their wallets and money from their budget envelopes. 2. Students stand in line to place a verbal order—use the mode of communication specified in the IEP. 3. Students place the order with the cashier and pay for the purchase. 4. Students move to "Pick up Orders Here." 5. Students find empty seats.

	Snack Shop (continued)

Set Up for Table Service Method:	1. Put tablecloths on the tables and napkins and silverware at seats
	2. Place menus near the door
	3. Set up table for food and drinks
	   a. food cut up in servings and put on plates
	   b. drinks poured
	   c. trays to carry food
	5. Designate a location for cashier
	   a. cash register
	   b. money
	   c. mints
	6. Assign servers (a good place to use peer helpers or practice a vocational skill)
	   a. order blanks
	   b. weekly selections
	   c. pencils

Directions:	Students who are the patrons need wallets/purses and money from their budget envelopes. 1. Have students who are the patrons wait in groups outside of the designated area. 2. Have one student be the hostess and seat patrons and give them menus. 3. Have a server come around for drink orders. 4. When drinks are served, the server takes the snack order. 5. Have the server serve food. 6. Have the srver gives students the bill when they are finished. 7. Have students use a tip card to determine tip amount. 8. Have students go to the cashier and pay for the bill.

Mini-Mart	
Purpose:	To practice shopping skills
Skills:	*Academic:* money skills, reading prices, measurements, comparisons *Communication:* making requests, following verbal directions *Social:* seeking assistance, appropriate manners
Materials:	Snack foods, soda cans, 2-liter soda bottles, cups, sandwich bags for snacks, pencils, erasers, paper, grab bag items, coupons for free-time activities, cash register, money, price tags, workers' vests, name tags
Set Up:	Once a week 1. Set up two display tables. 2. Organize grab bag items in small plastic bins for easy storage. 3. Set up cash register, money. 4. Arrange for peer helpers.
Directions:	1. Students who are the patrons get their wallets and money from their budget envelopes. 2. Teacher, assistants, or peers help students count their money and determine what they can afford. 3. When it is a student's turn, he or she tours the store to decide what to buy. 4. Students select items. 5. Students go to the cashier to pay for the items.

Gift Shop	
Purpose:	To practice shopping skills and coordinate with the reward system similar to Mini-Mart, but more motivating items
Skills:	*Academic:* money skills, reading prices, measurements, comparisons *Communication:* making requests, following verbal directions *Social:* Seeking assistance, appropriate manners
Materials:	Items to purchase, such as folders, tablets, pencils, pens, trinkets, tiny games, snack foods, soda cans, 2-liter soda bottles, cups, sandwich bags for snacks, pencils, erasers, paper, coupons for free-time activities, cash register, money, price tags, worker's vests, name tags
Set Up:	Once a month—Same as Mini-Mart
Directions:	Same as Mini-Mart

Post Office	
Purpose:	To practice post office skills in the classroom or when the post office is a long distance from school
Skills:	*Academic:* money skills, minimal reading, following written directions, basic writing skills *Communication:* making requests, following verbal directions *Social:* appropriate manners
Materials:	Postage stamps (generic or copies), envelopes, stationery, money, cash register, sign with samples of stamps, post office signs, wallet, money for budget envelope
Set Up:	1. Unit may be done as a separate unit, weekly, or in conjunction with the Mini-Mart. 2. If done with the Mini-Mart, complete the post office skills first as a budgeting item. (Going to the Mini-Mart first may be too tempting, not allowing enough money to participate in post office activities). 3. Have a table designated for writing supplies and stamps. 4. Have a post office box with slots labeled "Local" and "Out of Town."
Directions:	1. Students pick out their stamp designs and writing materials. 2. Students pay for their purchases. 3. Students store their items in the notebook—they will be used to write their parents or grandparents a letter and address an envelope with return and forwarding address (preaddressed if necessary) (see Appendix C7 for support with letter writing). 4. Students place mail in the correct slot on the next trip to the post office.
How To Make Stamps:	Use computer-generated graphics. Use a sheet of labels in lieu of printer paper. With proper spacing, print the graphic stamp on the label. Cut apart and use like self-adhesive stamps.
How To Make a Mail Box:	Use the flat side of two styrofoam egg cartons. Cut slots in each section to represent the different areas (Local or Out of Town) and then put baskets in each section to catch the mail. To make the top rounded, take a poster board strip (the same width as the box) and bend it in a half circle. The sides are two half circles cut out and taped to the strip. Spray paint the box and use an eagle symbol on the sides.

Town Theater	
Purpose:	To practice movie theater skills prior to visiting a theater
Skills:	*Academic:* money skills, reading a menu board for prices, reading a movie theater board for ticket prices *Communication:* making needs and desires known *Social:* food manners in a theater and at the snack bar
Materials:	Movie theater sign announcing the movie and ticket price, cash register, money for change, tickets, snack bar sign announcing snacks, drink flavors, sizes and prices, bowls, popcorn, soda/drinks, paper cups, VCR, vests, and name tags
Set Up:	1. Put a table near the door for the cash register. 2. Fill the register with $1 bills and tickets, made on the computer with the movie name and date typed on it. Cut out the tickets, then cut a small slit where the ticket is going to be ripped. 3. Set up chairs in rows with an aisle between. 4. Put the VCR in front of the chairs. 5. Set up two tables for the snack bar. 6. Display snack bar signs with objects representing the different items available (i.e., large cup vs. small cup). 7. Have the soda and popcorn ready in the back.
Directions:	1. Have students wait in the hall until the ticket box office opens. 2. Begin the sale of tickets at the designated time. 3. Have students go to the ticket person who will rip their tickets in half and then direct them to the correct section to choose their seats. 4. Show one half of the video. 5. Allow the students to go to the snack bar to buy snacks and drinks by placing their orders with the snack bar attendant. The attendant gets the order ready and hands it to the cashier, to whom the student pays the money. 6. Show the second half of the movie. 7. Comment on the students' behavior during procedures.

Conclusion

This chapter considered the community skills needed by all students. Access by all students was emphasized by ensuring that the general curriculum contains community skills. The chapter also looked at the curriculum for students with support needs and how it is managed in the school and classroom. Transition outcomes were described because they drive the IEP.

Examples of IEP goals and benchmarks that include CBI as a method were offered to help the reader understand how the whole planning and implementation process are integrated. A collection of "How-to-Teach" examples of specific skills was presented to give teachers concrete ideas about implementing CBI in the classroom. Chapter 5 describes how to move the instruction from the classroom and how to implement the skills in the community.

Forms Related to Chapter 4—Appendix C

Appendix C1   Sample of Leisure Activities

Appendix C2   Sample of Basic Skills

Appendix C3   Activities and Worksheets

Appendix C4   Sample Behavior System

Appendix C5   Classroom Banking

Appendix C6   Sample Lesson Plans

Appendix C7   Letter Writing

Points to Ponder

1. What content area skills in the general curriculum utilize the concepts of community-based instructional strategies?

2. Is there a place in the educational programming for teaching appropriate leisure activities? Why does the literature support leisure education, and how can teachers justify spending limited instructional time on recreational activities?

3. When considering transition outcomes, how does a team made up of family, educators, and agency personnel decipher the most appropriate long-range outcomes for students with support needs?

4. When developing the IEP's transition plan, how does a team integrate postsecondary outcomes, IEP goals, and curricular demands into one workable plan?

Reference

Brolin, D.E. (1997). *Life centered career education: A competency based approach* (5th ed.). Arlington, VA: Council for Exceptional Children.

Pugach, M.C., & Warger, C.L. (Eds.). (1996). *Curriculum trends, special education, and reform*. New York: Teachers College Press.

Suggested Reading

Brolin, D.E. (1997). *Life centered career education*. Arlington, VA: Council for Exceptional Children.

McDonnell, L.M., & McLaughlin, M.J. (Eds.). (1997). *Education one and all: Students with disabilities and standards-based reform.* Washington, DC: National Academies Press.

Moon, M.S. (1994). *Making school and community recreation fun for everyone.* Baltimore, MD: Paul H. Brookes.

Morse, T.E., & Schuster, J.W. (2000). Teaching elementary students with moderate intellectual disabilities how to shop for groceries. *Exceptional Children, 66,* 273-288.

Pennsylvania guidelines for secondary transition for students with disabilities. (1999). Pennsylvania Department of Education, Bureau of Special Education.

Pierangelo, R., & Crane, R. (1997). *Complete guide to special education transition services.* West Nyack, NY: The Center for Applied Research in Education.

Sitlington, P.L., Clark, G.M., & Kolstoe, O.P. (2000). *Transition education and services for adolescents with disabilities* (3rd ed.). Boston: Allyn & Bacon.

Szymanski, E.M., & Parker, R.M. (Eds.). (1996). *Work and disability.* Austin,TX: Pro-Ed.

Chapter 5

Independence in All Aspects of the Community

In this chapter . . .

- ◆ How are general curriculum concepts taught in the community?

- ◆ How can students with extensive or pervasive support needs transfer skills from the classroom to the community?

- ◆ What are the natural environments in which CBI can take place?

- ◆ What strategies promote independence in natural environments?

- ◆ What nonacademic independent skills do students need in the community?

- ◆ What strategies promote independence in all aspects of the community?

- ◆ What self-determination strategies do students need in the community?

How Are General Curriculum Concepts Taught in the Community?

This manual has established that state, subject area, and school district standards drive the curriculum. In addition, the accountability processes surrounding those standards make it imperative that districts keep a keen eye on content to be sure it meets the standards and assessment criteria. The method of instruction applied in schools and the academic freedom of teachers—to use creative strategies, stimulating materials, and a wide range of professional resources—opens the door for instruction to occur anywhere that a valuable learning opportunity presents itself. A brief discussion of traditional out-of-school locations that could be used in urban, suburban, or rural school districts includes the following:

1. On-site instruction, laboratory classes

2. Business partnerships, school-to-work projects

3. Career days

4. Individual projects

5. Advanced educational opportunities

On-Site Instruction, Laboratory Classes

Most students participate in science classes that go outside to a pond or creek to study simple forms of life. Not every student, by virtue of location, has gone to a state legislative session or mechanized dairy farm. Taking advantage of local opportunities enriches the curriculum for all students, as does looking for expanded opportunities to conduct class in area businesses, or off-campus sites, such as a library or planetarium. Teachers evaluate the benefits of leaving the classroom in relationship to standards-based content, time, and cost issues. Whenever possible, all students should receive real-world, hands-on experience.

Business Partnerships, School-to-Work Projects

As mentioned earlier, community partnerships influence the curriculum in a practical way. Those who develop standards consult with the business world about how to best prepare workers, managers, and executives. Advising schools about skills and knowledge needed for success, speaking in schools about the services or products provided in specific businesses, and providing on site experiences for high school students prior to graduation are the most common contributions made by local businesses. Schools often seek financial or other resource support from businesses. Investments from large profit-oriented or nonprofit organizations greatly enhance the school program. Administrators typically work on the resource and curricular input of business, while classroom teachers work on arrangements and content that can be mutually shared in the best environment.

School-to-work opportunities are based on individual students' needs and interests. Small groups may travel to participate in work exploration activities or work experiences. Business partnerships make a continuum of in-school and on-location options available to meet students' interests. As students clarify their career goals and want more direct knowledge of specific business, they may engage in cooperative learning experiences directly within a business. In these cases, they receive curricular content on site or in the classroom and may secure part-time employment, as well. There are many benefits to the use of cooperative experiences and apprenticeships. They include a combination of training and entry-level paid work. Once considered a training ground for vocational trades, apprenticeships have expanded into many professional occupations.

Career Days

Schools have limited space for large-scale presentations such as job fairs. The cafeteria is in use most of the day, and the gymnasium is active from before school to late evening.

Locating career information at conference centers, community colleges, or corporate buildings not only gives the necessary footage for displays but also creates a career-oriented atmosphere. There are spaces for small group seminars and noteworthy speaker sessions. Interactive vendor displays or higher education recruiters have more space for interviews and to show the diversity of opportunities they offer. Basing postschool awareness and exploration programs outside of the school facility allows students choice and the benefits of numerous experts in a wide collection of disciplines.

Individual Projects

Schools that require service learning or senior projects expect that these projects will be done independently outside of school. Service learning usually involves volunteerism in the community that could range from direct services to environmental projects. Service learning may be done in small groups, whereas senior projects are structured, individual activities that relate to a student's area of interest or career goals. Both of these activities involve partnerships, arrangements, family support, and help with preparing data, reports, and presentations. Outcomes of the projects are totally dependent on community cooperation and have long-lasting impact on both students and those they serve.

Advanced Educational Opportunities

When students have the opportunity to attend advance placement classes at a local college, there is an obvious relationship of community interaction and the curriculum. School districts that do not have direct access to colleges may investigate government programs, adult training facilities, and distance learning to provide students with enrichment activities and to determine which advanced educational experiences will help students meet higher standards or begin specialization in a field. Teachers need to look at students' interests and their background. All stakeholders—the student, family, teacher, administrators, and college personnel—have valuable input into what type of learning would benefit the high school student and how much time should be spent in other settings. Students who spend part of the day out of school in advanced settings may be deprived of beneficial experiences with same-age peers. Therefore, total student involvement and thoughtful team discussions help students and their families seek appropriate educational opportunities.

How Can Students With Extensive or Pervasive Support Needs Transfer Skills From the Classroom to the Community?

The fading of classroom activities and the transition into community settings accentuates the continuous focus of CBI. Instruction in the community occurs concurrently with all other forms of instruction. Teachers plan activities that will ensure that students apply the skills they have learned and increase their autonomy in solving problems. For example, support materials should not differ greatly from the classroom to the community. When planning activities and prompts, teachers usually prefer a least-to-most procedure. This method helps students increase their skills but does not create dependency. Students need prompts that are portable, manageable, and easy to use. In the long run, students who do not rely on picture cards, calculators, and obvious signs of support are more motivated and confident. For students who need adaptations to participate or to increase their independence, teachers can work prompts into students' overall instructional plans. Attention to final outcomes early in the transition program makes the process smooth and effective.

Structured Transition Into the Community

Moving teaching into the community requires a structured, systematic plan. The plan creates opportunities to take isolated classroom skills and activities and use them on a larger scale. Because the classroom program is formulated around what is needed in the community, much of the transition process evolves before leaving the school building. How a student uses a specific skill the last day in the classroom should be very close to how the student uses that skill the first day in the community. At that point, the process of applying techniques and fading prompts begins.

Teachers need to consider the process of transferring skills from the classroom to the community, not the specific skills to be transferred. On the last day an activity is performed in the classroom, students can rehearse what was done and how that task was performed. Students should explain what they think will be different in the community. Teachers can elicit responses such as, "The site is very large. There will be many people. The cashier may be busy and ask us to move quickly." These discussions emotionally prepare students for pressures that occur outside of the comfortable classroom. The questions and answers may vary, but drawing attention to a few differences helps to prevent undue surprises.

On the first day of a specific community outing, while still in the classroom, teachers should move beyond the students' emotional concerns to direct instruction about what should occur on site. Items to review include the skills practiced in the classroom, safety rules, a checklist of items needed for task performance, a list of items needed to take (a purse or wallet, identification card, tissues), assignment of groups and supervisors, specific directions, and clarifications of questions. After a few repetitions of the intended activity, students should begin to lead the transition discussion. The need to add specific information always exists, but overall, the goal is to get into the community to practice skills with the best preparation possible (see Appendix D1).

Independent Performance in the Community

What do secondary students with support needs do in the community when they are not in an instructional situation? Do they participate in school and community activities? Or go places with their families? Do they venture out alone? These times present the opportunity to judge true independence in the community. Assessment of these times occurs more by what the students do nonchalantly than by deliberate actions. True independence emerges when young adults go about their affairs with little or no attention to the process they or others use to participate in activities.

Adolescents acquire exposure to the outside world at increasingly younger ages. When parents and teachers display confidence that a young adult demonstrates age-appropriate safety and adaptive skills, independent performance emerges. This does not mean the end of repeated practice, refinement, generalization, or maintenance. It means that problem-solving becomes a daily activity and more complicated situations occur naturally. Spontaneous situations, such as a bus not coming at the scheduled time, or a specific product being out-of-stock in the grocery store, offer opportunities for students to experience everyday occurrences.

Consider this example. Jack was participating in a job project at a snack bar near school. The designated time to meet the job coach was 12:30. As the class completed lunch, in the busy cafeteria, the paraeducator instructed Jack to throw away his lunch bag and wait at the door to be escorted to the meeting place where the coach would be waiting. Jack threw away his lunch, then proceeded to leave school by another door, travel three blocks to the snack bar, do his job, and start back to school. In the meantime, the job coach determined that Jack was more than reasonably late. She called the teacher who began looking for Jack immediately. The paraeducator was frantic at the thought of the possibilities. Clearly, Jack did not follow instructions and safety was an issue. Fortunately, Jack traveled safely and effectively. He applied all of his travel and work skills and returned to school after completing his job.

In retrospect, after having sternly emphasized the consequences of not following directions, the teacher and job coach determined that it was time to give Jack more independence. They progressed to doing stationed observations along the way instead of the totally escorted procedure they had always followed. This was a tough lesson for everyone, but also showed that Jack was ready for and capable of more independence.

What Are the Natural Environments in Which CBI Can Take Place?

Every place an individual travels is a natural environment. This section includes a listing of those locations where CBI most frequently takes place. When a parent or student requests a location specific to a student's needs, the teacher tries to incorporate the location as a training site. By the high school years, CBI should be very personalized to include local establishments that the student and parent feel will enhance independence upon graduation. Residential and leisure locations comprise many of the special requests that teachers receive. A general list of locations used frequently throughout the middle and high school years includes the following:

1. Grocery stores, drug stores, department stores

2. Services: post office, libraries, laundromats, restaurants, public transportation, farmer's markets, government agencies, advocacy agencies

3. Recreational areas: parks, health clubs, sports stadiums, shopping malls, amusement areas

If these locations are natural environments outside of school, why would schools include only a few of those locations for CBI? The purpose of conducting CBI within the school curriculum and school day is to increase students' success. Therefore, students must learn about these locations as part of their school program.

Grocery Stores, Drug Stores, Department Stores

Major chain stores provide several advantages. The most relevant advantages include the consistency of layout and the system of pricing. When locating items by using aisle signs, students learn the categories and items included in those categories. When determining pricing, students know where to obtain the price and how to read the actual price of the item. For example, some stores list a price per quantity. A half gallon of ice cream may have the quart price listed first, then the actual price of the half gallon. Students must determine the correct price for the item and use that in their learning activities. After mastering major chain stores, the student will then have skills that can transfer to privately owned stores specific to the locality.

Services: Post Office, Government Agencies, Restaurants, Libraries, Public Transportation, Laundromats, Farmer's Markets, Advocacy Agencies

These locations may have consistent characteristics or may have unique arrangements. Government offices, post offices, and fast food restaurants frequently have similar layouts. Libraries and public transportation at various locations have many items in common, such as staff located behind counters ready to help patrons. Laundromats, local restaurants, farmer's markets, and advocacy agencies could look totally different depending on the town. The use of these locations also varies in frequency. A young adult may use public transportation daily to travel to school or work. Libraries, farmer's markets, and advocacy agencies could be visited on occasion. Certainly, the need of the individual to be familiar with the use of the service determines its emphasis when receiving instruction in the community.

Recreational Areas: Parks, Health Clubs, Sports Stadiums, Shopping Malls, Amusement Areas

Recreation training represents an important part of transition planning. The locations mentioned above comprise only a partial list of recreational sites to visit when addressing leisure skills. The layout and use of unique locations varies greatly and requires direct instruction. Personal preference in recreational activities, as well as enjoyability, affordability, and availability, must determine whether they become part of a student's scheduled CBI plan. Students and families create the recreational list that they feel will lead to interesting and productive activities for young adults. It is important to emphasize that some families prefer to teach leisure skills at home and have the school program concentrate on academic skills taught through CBI (see Appendix D2).

What Strategies Promote Independence in Natural Environments?

To be effective, strategies for teaching independence in natural environments must include many factors. Teachers need to decide what locations expose students to a variety of experiences, then formulate strategies that introduce and reinforce students' skills. These strategies contribute to a strong relationship between skills and independence. Whenever possible, the general curriculum should address skills in the community, and students should support each other in different locations.

Activities for Specific Locations

Many skills generalize to every location a person visits, such as entrance ways, exits, some type of aisle indicators, and the need to interact with employees of the location. Other skills, such as determining correct postage to mail a package, represent skills specific to one location. The process used to teach general and specific skills can be modeled or demonstrated for students requiring limited support or task analyzed for students needing pervasive support. A consistent strategy to familiarize students with a process that they can learn and implement to self-instruct when a place is unfamiliar may be one of the most valuable community skills a student can learn. Examples of activities in common locations to enhance the learning of students requiring support needs include the following:

Grocery Store. Teachers should split the class into groups, determined by the number of adults available, before traveling to the specific grocery store. At the store, students will practice the different skills they learned in the classroom by buying items needed for an afternoon cooking class. Teachers can assess the skills before returning to the classroom. The next travel session, students can practice the same skill or proceed to a new skill.

Restaurant. Begin by visiting restaurants familiar to the students, such as a fast food place, and progress through breakfast and lunch. Then, visit family, table service restaurants to have students practice ordering, paying, and tipping. Finally, the class can go to family buffet restaurants. The number of visits at each location may depend on budget as much as the need for practice. Also, family preferences and local availability influence restaurant training.

Post Office. Parents can provide a mailing list of five or more special people. Students create a card, either by hand or on the computer. Teachers can have students address the envelope as part of classroom instruction. When the class travels to a local post office, students purchase a stamp and mail the card.

Leisure Activity. At least once a week, students should have an enjoyable and affordable recreation experience. School will offer many such activities; however, students in secondary schools need to look beyond school for future leisure activities. A list of some activities includes swimming, movies, and sports. Recreation and leisure are part of the transition plan. Using CBI to foster those experiences is an appropriate way to increase students' opportunities and interests. As higher academic skills are being demanded of all students, teachers will have to make time to focus on leisure activities at least once a month.

What Nonacademic Independent Skills Do Students Need in the Community?

Families often discover that difficulties arise, not from weak academic skills, but from the inability to process situations and make decisions. Without question, academic skills increase opportunities in the workforce and add independence with daily tasks. Nonetheless, while proficiency with academics progresses, the young adult can also participate in many interactive experiences. Students with support needs face the same constant need to correctly perceive and interpret social situations as do all individuals. They must make easy choices and major decisions. Simple problems call for simple solutions. On the other hand, major situations take expanded reflection. Throughout these experiences, the individual must remain alert and composed, not always an easy task. This discussion emphasizes the need for students to receive instruction in the areas of reading situations, making decisions, solving problems, and monitoring themselves. Next, some strategies to address each area provide the teacher with a starting point to teach skills that prepare the student for unexpected incidents.

Reading the Situation

Students frequently misread social situations. They can misinterpret circumstances if they do not receive direct instruction. Students continually ask themselves mental questions that help them to respond to the situation appropriately. Am I welcomed in this discussion my classmates are having about last week's ball game? Is the teacher indirectly asking me to help my partner? I see someone's excitement level rising. Is this a situation that will defuse or escalate? The number of situations students must perceive and interpret presents an endless list of times when interpretation affects actions, which then affects the reaction of others. Adults seem to perform this reflection subconsciously. Part of the instruction in CBI includes helping students, especially those needing support, to ask themselves questions and answer those questions before acting. Success with the process depends on perception, the ability to take information from the environment, and a correct interpretation of what is happening. Students participate in many activities that allow them to practice perceiving visual and auditory information. Social situations require the same process, but with a much more sophisticated repertoire of responses.

Making Decisions

Making both quick decisions and reflective responses direct the course of students' everyday life. Starting with easy choices—one desirable, one undesirable—gives students confirmation that they have a choice. Moving on to deciding between two desirable choices presents more difficulty. Positive results occur when students learn the long-range effects of their choices and they understand the true challenge associated with making decisions. Teachers create the opportunity to make decisions in structured settings that allow students to play out the consequences of their decisions. Teachers can help students understand that positive and negative consequences result from their decisions, and that, in many cases, they cannot go back and change their minds.

Solving Problems

Inevitably, unforeseen problems arise. Most problems occur in simple and typical situations such as, "The store I intended to visit is closed for inventory." In which case, through a logical process, the individual can decide to either come back another day or go to another store with similar products. Other problems may take weeks of careful deliberation to solve. For example, "Where do I live until a spot opens in an independent living arrangement?" In this case, there is a chain of events that influences the solution. In the younger grades, teachers present the standard problem-solving process that includes stating the problem, looking at variables, brain-storming solutions, weighing options, choosing a solution, evaluating the decision, and continuing on to solve the problem or going back for an alternative solution. Later, students receive practice applying the process to situations in their lives. At times, it is difficult to separate problem-solving from decision-making. Decision-making can be a simple choice, or, in more involved cases, decision-making is a part of the problem-solving process. At first, both decision-making skills and problem-solving skills need to be taught separately; later the combination of skills helps students respond to the demands of the situation (see Appendix D3).

Self-Monitoring

Throughout the process of daily activities, adults must maintain a stable emotional state and make appropriate responses. To provide effective reactions, individuals must regulate their own behaviors. This alone can be a goal for students who have social and emotional needs related to a disability. Students of all levels need to know that emotions are healthy, and they must be able to recognize their own emotional behaviors. In addition, self-control is impor tant. Students with emotional concerns often need intensive instruction on regulating their self-control. Self-monitoring describes a method of self-questioning and self-evaluation that gives students a strategy to continually evaluate the effectiveness of their responses to situations. Other people in the environment naturally contribute feedback. Individuals use the skills learned through reading the situation to provide themselves with feedback about their response to a particular incident. The cyclical effect of social behaviors needed in the community represents the complicated process of teaching young adults with support needs how to perceive, interpret, and effectively respond to every situation.

What Strategies Promote Independence in All Aspects of Community?

In the classroom, role-playing, direct instruction, and supportive materials help teachers expose students to problems that could surface when they are in the community. When in the community, staged problems are difficult to construct. Teachers may try to create artificial situations that call for problem-solving skills. However, teachers often prefer to wait until an unexpected incident occurs, then use direct instruction to talk the student through a structured process that leads to an appropriate action in that setting. In the community, unexpected situations occur frequently, which enables students to have spontaneous and varied practice.

Direct Instruction

Teachers rely heavily on direct instruction as an obvious and effective way to involve students in skill acquisition. Consistent and directive comments help students to sequence behaviors and internalize skills. There are some situations in which waiting for students to discover the appropriate response to a situation may be unsafe or extremely time consuming. Verbal directions, modeling, and guided practice make direct instruction an appropriate intervention for many situations. Of course, if there is time and the opportunity for a student to discover how to complete a task without intervention, that process should be allowed to occur.

Role-Playing

Once thought to be a way to demonstrate emotions; role-playing illustrates a way to model, practice, and assess social and problem-solving skills. To model, or teach an appropriate example, the instructional and support staff can role-play any number of situations. Two adults can demonstrate appropriate responses to questions or situations that may occur in the community. On the other hand, students can be given a situation and asked to role-play the solution. Teachers can use this session to evaluate progress or to check student understanding. For less imaginative students, adults may act out a scenario and have the students evaluate the appropriateness of a behavior.

Resources

Depending on the students' level, written lists or a poster displayed in the classroom will give students reminders of materials they need before an excursion. Students with extensive or pervasive support needs may require the use of commercial or computer-generated picture cards. Repeated practice with standard routines and supportive materials enhances the success for the student (see Appendix D4). A list of teacher made materials could include

- Written or color-coded cards for items needed in the community.

- Picture cards of generic items gained from coupons and store circulars.

- Prewritten restaurant orders.

- Predetermined lists or pictures of items a student wants to order, or phrases such as, "One stamp please," to support a student with language difficulties.

What Self-Determination Strategies Do Students Need in the Community?

Self-determination, the best practice of preparing individuals to control their own situations, combines the concepts of "free choice" and "self-advocacy." Self-determination represents more than striving for rights; it involves making decisions and acquiring the skills needed to make good choices that will affect the future. By direct example and modeling, teachers can begin to help students learn how to guide their lives in the direction they choose. Personal acceptance begins very early. Direct communication is a developmental skill that is actually more natural for very young children than it is for older students who may be self-conscious. Students who demonstrate autonomy and confidence in their methods to achieve satisfaction provide peer models for other students who need methods of being accepted, respected, and heard. The items listed below comprise an ongoing focus within the adapted or alternative curriculum. Recognizing these areas and instructing students how to manage the skills begins very early in the educational careers of all students. The following areas support students as they strive for independence:

1. Seeking immediate assistance.

2. Self-knowledge, personal accommodations.

3. Personal and citizen rights.

4. Obtaining services.

5. Augmentative communication and assistive devices.

Seeking Immediate Assistance

Most situations do not require the assistance of a professional, rather, young adults simply need help completing a task. Asking someone seated near them in class starts the process of understanding their own needs and developing the confidence to seek help. Knowledge of safety and emergency services required in a crisis, such as dialing 911, is important, but used so rarely that it should not be overemphasized. The need for daily, personal support with frequently experienced situations gives young adults the opportunity to assess their own needs and strive to get those needs met independently.

To prepare students for emergencies, teachers should equip them with identification information, have them practice repeating personal information that would help them to get assistance, and memorize safe pedestrian, stranger, and passenger travel rules. Families, peers, and classmates can help, too. Early in the educational process, community service personnel can demonstrate when and how students should seek assistance. All resources available should be used to ensure that individuals in need of support know safe practices and how to acquire assistance.

Self-Knowledge, Personal Accommodations

Medical conditions, such as needing an inhaler for asthma or insulin for diabetes, dictate that students know their needs and be able to articulate them in a timely fashion to promote their own health. Individuals with physical, mental, and emotional needs should also be able to state what they need for success. This involves self-knowledge of personal needs associated with individual circumstances. Students need knowledge of their personal characteristics and the ability to seek what they need to support learning and interpersonal interactions; this ability should be as basic as understanding their medical needs. When teaching self-awareness, teachers can present facts about student needs and direct communication. For example, if a student needs a menu read to them, they can learn to say, "What are your most popular dishes?" Positive requests are more productive than stating facts like, "I am a poor reader." On the other hand, if an individual with mobility needs cannot navigate a ramp in a wheelchair, a direct request such as, "Could you please push me up the ramp?" is all that is needed.

Does the individual need to sit near the front of the classroom to enhance concentration? Is longer time needed for a test? Will a calculator make him or her an independent shopper? Is a long skirt with velcro fasteners the best type of clothing for a lady who uses a wheelchair? These considerations should be as commonplace as needing glasses or orthodontics. Teachers start with very young children to instill the notion that asking for these items is a necessity, not an infirmity. Helping students learn how to make clear, direct requests enables them to receive assistance and continue with the activity at hand. Nevertheless, the value of independence must be highlighted so children do not get into the habit of asking for more help than necessary and become overly dependent in the process.

Personal and Citizen Rights

Educational legislation instituted procedural safeguards that clearly state how the school system honors a student's and family's educational rights. Interestingly enough, in the outside world, freedom does not mean doing whatever a person feels like doing. Equal rights, and the rights to be safe and pursue dreams, surface as a challenge to all subgroups of society. In some respects, society has not done a good job of teaching its citizens the expanse of rights they are entitled to and the approach they should use to ensure those rights are preserved. The educational system begins with teaching the concept of personal rights, but the total understanding of what that means must continue well into adulthood. Knowledge of personal rights and the responsibility to utilize personal liberties in appropriate ways represents lifelong learning for all citizens. It must begin in primary grades and continue each time the question surfaces.

Obtaining Services

One of the most encouraging experiences for people working in a field that serves individuals with support needs has been the implementation of the Americans with Disabilities Act. Much work has yet to be done, but the effort to open services to all citizens is progressing. Before they leave the school system, students need deliberate, hands-on experiences that enable them to understand how to access services, plan for, and obtain everyday conveniences. Students need to be their own self-advocates when they meet challenges in obtaining services. If support is necessary to obtain a service, students need to learn how to access that support. Part of direct instruction in the community teaches students methods of effectively obtaining services.

Augmentative Communication and Assistive Devices

Support in evaluating and acquiring assistive technology can be initiated through school support personnel who are familiar with grant opportunities, the capabilities of assistive technology, and the individual making the request. Communication and assistive technology is expensive and complicated. Choosing the most functional device for an individual takes a team, including the individual who needs the device, the family, and professionals familiar with the array of devices on the market. Functional technology that helps individuals be more independent and influential over their environment and allows more social interaction is well worth the time spent researching the most appropriate devices.

Conclusion

The general curriculum includes many skills that may benefit from instruction that takes place in the community. A district's decision to implement CBI depends on standards and assessment issues. For students with support needs, transferring skills from the classroom to the community is a basic part of the comprehensive instructional process. Once students with support needs leave the classroom and enter the community, they need a new set of skills. Making a smooth transition, developing strategies to support the students, and providing varied practice in community locations increases students' abilities to face similar and unexpected situations. Teachers develop an array of strategies and supportive material to help students acquire independence. In addition to independent living skills, an individual who lives and works in the community needs safety, problem-solving, and self-determination skills to be interdependent as well as independent.

Forms Related to Chapter 5—Appendix D

Appendix D1   The Transition from Classroom to Community

Appendix D2   Task Analysis Particular to Specific Community Sites

Appendix D3   Problem Solving Areas

Appendix D4   Picture Preparation List

Points to Ponder

1. What aspects of your general curriculum would benefit from direct instruction in the community?

2. What process would work in the local district to help students transfer acquired classroom skills into independent community skills?

3. Compile a list of natural CBI locations close to the local school. Prioritize the list by frequency of use and interest level of the students.

4. What skills needed in the community, which are unnatural to simulate in the classroom, will help students with independent skills in most community locations?

5. How can teachers help students deal with unexpected situations?

6. What teaching and practice strategies work best for your students? Are they adaptable to community settings?

7. How do adults get needed assistance from strangers? What is the best way to teach polite assertiveness to students with support needs?

Suggested Reading

Brigance, A.H. (1995). *Life skills inventory.* North Billerica, MA: Curriculum Associates.

Brolin, D.E. (1995). *Career education: A functional life skills approach,* (3rd ed.). Englewood Cliffs, NJ: Merrill.

Ford, A., Schnorr, R., Meyer, L., Davern, L., Black, J., & Dempsey, P. (1989). *The Syracuse community-referenced curriculum guide.* Baltimore: Paul H. Brookes.

Pierangelo, R., & Crane, R. (1997). *Complete guide to special education transition services.* West Nyack, NY: The Center for Applied Research in Education.

Shure, M.B. (1992). *I can problem solve.* Champaign, IL: Research Press.

Sitlington, P.L., Clark, G.M., & Kolstoe, O.P. (2000). *Transition education and services for adolescents with disabilities.* Boston: Allyn & Bacon.

Westling, D.L. & Fox, L. (2000). *Teaching students with severe disabilities* (2nd ed.). Upper Saddle River, NJ: Merrill.

Chapter 6

Evaluation of Community-Based Instruction Programs

In this chapter . . .

◆ How is CBI proven successful?

◆ What assessment basics are relevant to the evaluation of CBI?

◆ What are the important evaluation questions to ask regarding CBI?

◆ How does a special education teacher set up an assessment process?

◆ What types of evaluation strategies are appropriate for CBI?

◆ How is assessment information translated into student achievement and program improvement?

◆ How is assessment information used to show accountability?

How Is CBI Proven Successful?

Students demonstrate independent skills in a variety of community settings. Teachers collect and present data that indicates steps students have mastered. This data proves the success of CBI. Good assessment and clear documentation gives teachers a visual representation that shows students and their families the beginning point, the ending point, and the student's progress between those points. Furthermore, administrators, school boards, and state evaluators want proof that a district's instruction meets standards and creates capable citizens. In addition, administrators care about the cost effectiveness of methods and want to be sure that the strategies lead to student achievement. This chapter helps teachers perform quick and effective techniques to evaluate student progress. The results of student assessment contribute to the larger district-level assessment of the CBI program.

Student Evaluation

Assessment of CBI skills occurs before, during, and after instruction. Assessment defines the exact areas of needed instruction; as discussed in Chapter 3, suggests sequence and priorities; helps to create the plan for intervention; and dictates content, location, and intensity of instruction. In addition, the assessment process provides daily feedback about student progress (formative evaluation), effectiveness of teaching strategies, and final evaluation of ultimate performance (summative evaluation). Without a systematic assessment plan, teachers have little evidence that the student has learned the stated skills or that the instructional strategies and techniques have improved student performance.

Program Evaluation

Many factors go into producing desired results. Data from the teacher provide crucial information. Done correctly, a final step in the evaluation of students would produce a graph indicating individual student progress and overall class progress. These two items, provided from each teacher that uses CBI, help supervisors document program effectiveness. Other data, such as students living independently and retaining employment or parent and community satisfaction, indicate that extended outcomes are achieved. Effectiveness data and long-term outcomes information, when compared to overall cost, provide supervisors with evidence to present to higher-level administrators. Ultimately, effectiveness and productivity data influence the continuation of instructional programs.

What Assessment Basics Are Relevant to the Evaluation of CBI?

Assessing students' CBI skills and the entire CBI program requires a deliberate endeavor to implement an ongoing, systematic evaluation process. With student learning and independence as the ultimate goals, teachers must locate or develop proficient ways to indicate that students have acquired skills. Quick informative formats—which can transfer to progress charts and indicate that students achieve necessary skills—provide the teacher with information about student progress and instructional methods. Convenient and informative devices evolve from the teacher's repertoire of tools and a clear vision of what the use of those tools needs to reveal.

Kinds of Assessment

Assessment tools typically fall into two categories, formal and informal. Formal assessment tools, sometimes referred to as standardized tests, frequently call for group testing or individual testing by a specialist. These tests provide useful information about eligibility and placement. Formal assessments use strict guidelines for administering and scoring. They also dictate how to interpret the results. Evaluators compare results against a specific norm group and give information in relation to the group. Formal assessments also emphasize academic achievement. Results may give useful information for setting goals and making placement decisions for all students.

Informal tests gather information used to make instructional decisions. Special education teachers use teacher-made assessments that provide information directly related to current levels, progress reports, and effectiveness of strategies. The evaluation tools can be used by a variety of evaluators and may include checklists, observations, time samples, and curriculum-based assessments. Informal assessments look at behavior, social interaction, rate of progress, and mastery of goals. Teachers compare the results against an acceptable criteria rather than a norm group. The effective use of informal assessment tools varies greatly according to teacher experience and dedication to the process.

Informal assessment can be further broken down into formative and summative evaluations. Formative evaluation represents the frequent checking of skills to provide feedback and effective instruction. It takes many forms such as quizzes, verbal responses, projects, portfolios, or demonstrations. Summative evaluation occurs at the end of a large unit of study, grading period, semester, or school year. It indicates basic skills and knowledge and gives a general, overall performance level when compared to the initial entry-level skill and current performance. Summative evaluation, which occurs after long-term instruction, requires much less time than formative assessment and gives basic progress information with minimal details.

Because CBI addresses individual needs for specific students with disabilities, informal evaluation tools offer information that will affect instructional strategies and desired outcomes. Designing evaluation tools requires ongoing attempts at clearly defining the performance. Estimations do not provide the documentation that is necessary in the current educational climate. Therefore, the format of the evaluation tool fades in importance to the constant evaluation process and the ongoing recording of results. The figures offered with this chapter represent examples of teacher-made, teacher-friendly evaluation tools that assess student progress and program effectiveness.

Assessment for Transition Planning

Assessment for transition planning encompasses many facets. Transition plans address the areas of postsecondary education, employment, and independent living. Formal assessment in those areas compares the student to the general population. Then, a combination of informal checklists, interest inventories, surveys, and work samples indicate student preferences, family desires, work-related skills, and goal areas. As outlined in Chapter 3, the areas with the most intervention depend upon the students' intensity of needed services. Students with intermittent or limited support needs may require academic guidance to qualify for higher education or competitive employment, while students with extensive or pervasive support needs could indicate a need for employment skills and behaviors that promote independent living. If CBI can provide instruction in any area of intervention, then it should be used as a strategy to support transition planning. Therefore, assessment for transition planning occurs first. If transition assessment indicates that CBI would be a method to assist students in meeting their goals, then the CBI assessment would contribute to the evaluation of objectives stemming from transition goals.

Assessment for CBI

Assessment for CBI receives the same attention as other classroom assessments. The teacher creates the format and performs an assessment or directly supervises another person—perhaps a paraeducator—who administers assessments. The method becomes personalized to the students and the teacher. CBI assessments demand a great deal of effort in development and use. Nevertheless, CBI assessment remains crucial to the reporting of student progress and the evaluation of daily instruction. The transition portion of the IEP requires a statement of evaluation procedures. The method used to assess student performance in CBI areas directly affects the transition process and is recorded in appropriate sections of the IEP.

What Are the Important Evaluation Questions to Ask Regarding CBI?

Like all effective instructional strategies, CBI begins, changes, and ends with questions about what to teach, how to teach it, and whether the instruction was effective. This discussion focuses on the "What to teach?" component. Not unlike planning for any program, student and family desires rise to the top of the list of questions. Teacher information, knowledge of curriculum, and past experience then blend with the expectations expressed by the student and family. With those two stakeholders' wishes known, community members suggest skills needed from their business and social perspectives. Combined, the information gained through informal checklists drives the students program. Other areas of clarification and refinement appear after instruction begins (see Appendix B5).

Student and Family Checklist

Students' interests and preferences represent the most motivating and essential content of instruction. Parent requests, which are also crucial, should be an extension of the students' interests. Ideally, a list of transition outcomes will flow nicely into IEP goals, objectives, and specialized instruction. For example, Ken knew he wanted to work around cars. He envisioned driving the car into the garage for the mechanic. Ken's parents wanted him to be a mechanic, a job that takes extensive training. The transition team created a 3-year plan that included job awareness, basic auto maintenance tasks, and the skills of ordering uniforms, communicating with customers, and traveling to and from work. The initial checklist brought this planning sequence into reality.

If conflict arises between student and parent goals, time and effort goes into finding a common ground and writing a broad IEP that includes parts of both. Sincere teacher input may bridge the gap or help to sequence student desires and those of the family. Another example describes a student, with needs for support in cognitive areas, who wanted to drive. The student's goal of obtaining a driver's license reflects the wishes of typical teenagers. Her parents dreaded the thought of their daughter with extensive support needs getting behind the wheel and requested only public transportation training. Working as a member of the team, the teacher suggested beginning with pedestrian and public transportation and working on obtaining a driver's manual. By exploring the requirements for obtaining a learner's permit, the student became aware of the many stipulations of driving. The student's hopes to drive were not diverted, but she did recognize that it would be a long process. By gathering information, the school honored the wishes of both the student and the family.

Student checklists allow the program coordinator and teacher to know in what direction to proceed. Checklists provide basic data throughout the transition period. Students' and families' ideas change as students mature and broaden their knowledge base of possibilities. When teachers review previous results and compare them to results from current checklists, they can see both the increased sophistication of the students and new directions to pursue for ongoing instruction.

Community Checklists

Knowing the skills community business leaders think students should demonstrate can help narrow the perspective of the school staff member using CBI as an instructional strategy. When students visit specialized locations, what they learn is determined by the characteristics of the business. When concentrating on basic shopping skills, students and teachers need to know that all store managers do not have the same philosophy about their patrons. For example, grocery store employees check out customers and work behind specific counters. The grocer may expect individuals to make a concerted effort to locate items before they ask for help. On the other hand, in a drug store, a pharmacist may want patrons to seek help as soon as they cannot locate an item. Asking proprietors a few key questions will help teachers plan the order of visits and the instruction needed for each location prior to entering the community. Teachers can create a planning information checklist to save time and effort when providing direct instruction (see Appendix E1).

Teacher Checklists

Teachers observe students in many environments. Behaviors in those environments change due to the complexity of the situation, interpersonal interaction, and student ability. Teacher checklists provide valuable information about behavioral factors across school and community settings. District support team evaluators may ask teachers to do a checklist to compare it to one that parent(s) and the student have completed separately. Commercial inventories or professionally designed checklists glean teacher information.

Teachers usually document their personal thoughts as anecdotal notes rather than creating a checklist to ask themselves questions. As part of the planning team, teachers collect very specific information. If the situation calls for the same type of information about each student, a teacher may develop a checklist to show consistency and uniformity in what they report. Typically, teacher time is better spent gathering student, family, and community information than developing teacher checklists. Nevertheless, when a checklist saves time, teachers should consider developing one to obtain information that will help all team members get pertinent data that supports the student.

How Does a Special Education Teacher Set Up an Assessment Process?

Much time goes into the thought process of developing an assessment tool that precisely describes student achievement, meets the teacher's criteria, and is manageable while the teacher and student are involved in instruction. Commercial tools that assess the appropriate individual skills speed up the assessment process. However, teachers must remember that commercial assessment tools may clearly state the instructional sequence, but teachers must determine what portion of that sequence addresses the students' needs. The following explanation describes how a teacher thinks through this process and then develops, utilizes, interprets, and evaluates both student progress and the evaluation tool itself. This process should be used each time a teacher creates a unit of study. Once a process is perfected, there will be many opportunities to effectively apply the formats to new content.

The Assessment Process

Individual teachers approach assessment in several ways. Teachers may have worked with assessments in graduate programs or through undergraduate work. Some states dictate an assessment process that correlates with state assessment. Some districts want uniformity and formulate a districtwide process that teachers must use. The general sequence that follows offers teachers who are not experienced with assessment a starting point in planning and evaluating their own assessment processes.

1. Look at the unit of instruction.

2. Write down all of the skills used in the unit.

3. Make a task analysis for each skill, based on the specific needs of the class and individual students.

4. Make an assessment plan that details pretest, formative assessments throughout, and a posttest.

5. Develop a pretest to be used. To give clear information, this should exactly match the posttest used in the final evaluation.

6. Plan instruction.

7. Develop the assessment tools and data collection forms.

8. Complete instruction and formative assessment according to the plan.

9. Perform the posttest and record overall progress.

10. Transfer results of formative assessments to a progress graph.

11. Evaluate progress and learning patterns.

12. Write a summative evaluation.

Evaluating the Effectiveness of the Assessment Tool

Teachers should continue to evaluate the assessment tool even after completing the summative report. When in use, the ease of the tool will be evident. Teachers should try to stick with one tool during a unit; changing the tool midstream could frustrate the student and create an added burden for the teacher. After the instructional cycle ends, teachers can judge the effectiveness of the tool. A complete picture appears, and teachers can look at the overall process. The following list represents questions to ask about the assessment tool.

1. Was it easy to use?

2. Was it objective?

3. Would another assessment tool be more effective?

4. Does it clearly state student progress?

5. Was it easy to interpret?

How teachers answer these questions determines if the tool will become a consistent part of the assessment plan or if the assessment tool needs altering for further use. Time spent in this process can save valuable time later. Once these questions are answered, greater efficiency will occur both in the administration of assessment and in developing assessment tools.

What Types of Evaluation Strategies Are Appropriate for CBI?

Sophisticated evaluation procedures are developed through the painstaking efforts of a team of professionals over many years of adjustment and refinement. Ultimately, the bulk of the daily evaluation procedures falls upon the teaching team, which may include paraeducators, volunteers, and parents in addition to the teacher. A broad repertoire of methods enables the teacher to be precise and efficient in documenting and interpreting student progress. In addition, students respond differently to assessment; therefore, some forms of assessment may be "friendlier" and more reflective of student skills. Types of assessment tools include:

1. Data collection: checklists, anecdotal records, "clipboard assessment"

2. Performance and curriculum-based assessment

3. Portfolio assessment

4. Qualitative assessment (simple rubrics)

5. Performance graphs

Teachers usually study each of these types of assessment intensively while pursuing a degree. Few educators feel that they fully master the intricate details of total assessment. However, they do become skilled enough to use assessment procedures to gather information to determine student progress and assess teacher effectiveness.

Data Collection: Checklists, Anecdotal Records, "Clipboard Assessment"

Collecting data to make instructional decisions and verify that students are progressing forms the very basis of assessment. Teacher checklists provide quick, self-made lists of skills and criteria that a teacher, paraeducator, peer, or volunteer can use to evaluate a student on site throughout the instructional time in the community. "Clipboard assessment" simply means that the evaluator uses a clipboard for both a hard surface and a way to organize data sheets on students participating in CBI. Anecdotal notes are those quick references that teachers make as reminders or as clarification to data that may not offer the entire description of a student's performance. Teacher-made data sheets can be designed to fit a student's IEP or a basic curricular topic (see Appendixes E1, E2).

Performance and Curriculum-Based Assessment

Performance assessment and curriculum-based assessment refer to similar processes. Teachers use these methods to evaluate student progress as it directly relates to the curriculum. Teacher-made tests and observation checklists reflect the content the teacher emphasized during instruction; therefore, it is nearly impossible to find a perfect commercial assessment instrument. Assessment results derived from curriculum-based assessment give the teacher an immediate reflection of the instruction's effectiveness, what the student accomplished, and what instruction and practice must follow.

Portfolio Assessment

A portfolio represents a collection of items that show a student's accomplishments. As a rule, student portfolios reflect their work, show samples of process and outcomes over time, and can be evaluated based on criteria. Portfolios that reflect performance in the community may include checklists of skill acquisition; prompts used and faded; and anecdotal comments by community members, parents, and teachers. Portfolios contain references to individuals in the community who would verify the student's progress and success, or documents and pictures that show independent activities. Careful selection of information gives the portfolio its value. Students must update their portfolios to keep them current and reflective of their present skills. Portfolios may be used in CBI assessment to provide tangible evidence of skills that students accomplished and to provide documented proof of these skills from a variety of evaluation tools.

Qualitative Assessment (Simple Rubrics)

At times, a student demonstrates appropriate skills but not to the proficiency level needed to be independent. Rubrics give a comparative level of the skill that does not require an extended explanation. The rubric states various characteristics required to reach a specific performance level in such a way that the student and the evaluator know exactly what must be done to achieve each score. Teachers often use three- or five-point scales to show strength, average ability, or below average ability. It takes time for teachers to plan and develop the rubric, but, once created, it reduces the amount of writing needed while teachers work directly with their students. The use of a rubric also removes some of the subjectivity of qualitative evaluation and gives the evaluator a standard to use with each individual observed.

Uses of rubrics concentrate on material that must meet several standards, such as job applications, supply orders, portfolio collections, or other written documents. Written information must meet several quality standards. To complete a written item, information must be (a) correct, (b) complete, (c) placed in the correct area of the form, (d) neat and legible, (e) understood by the reader, and (f) consistent each time it is completed. The rubric to evaluate the written product describes competent performance, acceptable performance, and unacceptable performance through criteria ratings.

It takes extensive effort to develop a simple and precise rating rubric. Once achieved, the form is easy to use, very descriptive, and saves recording time. As with curriculum-based assessment, the rubric exactly matches the objectives being taught. Today's technology makes it much easier to locate rubrics for many areas. Web sites offer an array of usable ideas. However, it may be difficult to find commercial rubrics that are relevant to the individual student or classroom program. Once teachers master the process of developing rubrics, rubrics can be very useful in any area that requires subjective, qualitative evaluation (see Appendix E3).

Performance Graphs

Graphs represent a visual picture of overall individual performance or class progress. An individual student may not understand each item on a checklist or rubric but will recognize a line on a graph that progressively rises showing growth and positive performance. Teachers use lines of different colors to indicate student progress in several areas. They may also overlap student graphs to determine if the class as a whole is moving forward. Such a combined graph would be used for the teacher's own information or to share with a supervisor. Computer technology has greatly expedited the creation of graphs, charts, and visuals representations. Student performance reflects teacher accountability, making it essential that teachers use all tools available to document, interpret, and explain student performance (see Appendix E4).

How Is Assessment Information Translated Into Student Achievement and Program Improvement?

As stated earlier, teachers must develop formats that are convenient for all evaluators to use and that give quick, accurate, useful information. Ongoing assessment creates an abundance of paper and represents very small increments of learning. Graphs or charts help all stakeholders see the end results. Teachers' final documentation influences that information that is included on progress reports and helps educators make instructional decisions. The use of CBI gains continuity and improves proficiency as more and more student performances are scrutinized.

Interpreting and Utilizing Assessment Data

Once data are collected and reviewed, what do they mean? How should teachers use the data? What can teachers tell students and parents about student progress? What instructional information can teachers gain? If the evaluation tool examined the appropriate information, then teachers should be able to review the data and formulate an overall picture of a particular student or group of students. Each time data are collected, teachers should ask these questions:

1. Did the student show progress?

   If yes, continue. If no, make a judgment. Does the student need more practice, repeated demonstration, or different instruction?

2. How much more practice should be given using this technique?

3. Should the technique of instruction change?

4. Should methods, materials, outcomes, supports, or a combination of these be changed?

Each time data are collected, administrators should ask these questions:

1. Are students progressing?

2. Is the acquisition of skills and rate of progress directly linked to instruction?

3. Is the process cost effective?

If the gathered information forms a total picture, educators get an overall progress review. Once the total overview indicates rises and drops in performance, specific information can be used to suggest similarities or differences among students or whether the information conveys instructional information. Several individuals should review the data and come to their own conclusions. The consistency among evaluators will suggest the effectiveness of the process. A written report that shows narrative information about the results of the data can be the culmination of the interpretive process.

Some disciplines, such as school psychology, spend much training time using and interpreting assessment data. A transdisciplinary team approach helps produce an accurate interpretation of data. Obvious trends in performance, evidence of constant growth, and the effectiveness of instructional interventions can be determined by the overall representation of data. In the long run, teachers and administrators will improve their skills in interpreting assessment data and implement changes based on accurate reporting of student progress.

Implementing Change Based on Published and Active Research

So far, this discussion has been based solely upon individual teacher and classroom or school district programs. It must be stated that professionals spend much time and effort on what happens within the classroom, but what happens throughout the entire profession dictates trends and best practices. Professional development time often constitutes going to local inservice programs or attending conferences. Teachers should belong to organizations that publish research. Reading research and applying theory or methodology to personal instruction broadens teachers' perspectives and their repertoire of techniques for increasing student skills.

Contributing to the field by conducting active research allows teachers to offer strategies and techniques that have been successful with their students. By doing long-term studies or large sample data collection, teachers can show the success of specific strategies. Other professionals gain valuable ideas when viewing documented results from active research. Teachers should consider publishing data about successful programs and encourage others to do the same. Both students and teachers benefit from methods tried with similar populations in other locations.

Program Improvement

Program improvement spans all levels of the educational spectrum. Initially, it appears that program level changes rely mostly on administrative decisions. Undoubtedly, administrators bear the responsibility for fiscal, personnel, parent, community, and district-wide issues. Nevertheless, teacher input and commitment remains crucial to any systematic change. The decision to make changes comes from both long-term results of postgraduate data and ongoing interpretation of current student data. The ability to implement effective programming comes from a commitment by all stakeholders.

Administrators consider yearly information about cost factors, student needs, and long-term results. They also monitor elementary, middle, and high school programs for continuity and grade-level consistency to ensure a comprehensive program. The district's mission, philosophy, and upper-level administrative goals contribute to the vision and support of the CBI program throughout the K-12 and special education programs. Administrators use all the data available to them to create staff development programs that will address teachers' needs and create learning and performance outcomes for students.

Teachers represent the global picture of the program. A partial list of teacher experiences includes (a) concrete knowledge of student ability, (b) frequent interaction with local businesses, (c) study of graduate level research and conference attendance, (d) utilization of the full continuum of the curriculum, and (e) an understanding of district goals and administrative concerns. No other professional position requires such a total integration of all facets of the program. Despite their broad knowledge, teachers focus on the students in their classrooms. Teachers improve the system through productive planning and by teaching essential criteria. Therefore, change occurs through teachers' commitment and total involvement. To accomplish productive change, teachers need support to allow them time to concentrate and reflect on progress, methods, and future goals.

Staff development opportunities are one way to include teachers in program decisions. After-school meetings are not as productive. Teachers' thoughts are crowded with the day's events, tomorrow's preparation, and the duties they have waiting at home. Staff development program plans should include the needs of special education issues for secondary school students. A paid summer project gives teachers the opportunity to think about large-scale program development when they are planning their instruction for the coming school year.

How Is Assessment Information Used to Show Accountability?

Statewide assessments and alternative assessments for individuals who require extensive and pervasive support have been addressed several times throughout this book. Statewide assessments are a primary way to determine teachers' accountability and whether students have achieved standards. The general curriculum must include standards and state criteria in a large percentage of learning activities to show student improvement. The development of alternative assessments for students with support needs has not had the same influence. Concentrated work is still needed to make state alternative assessments, mostly given to students with extensive and pervasive support needs, a true indicator of accountability. Schools and districts can review formalized test information to determine students' exact areas of need.

Concentrating assessment efforts on informal measures allows for the most obvious forms of accountability to be utilized. Teachers' observations of students' performance improvement provides families with the accountability they desire. Caregivers who observe positive changes in students feel that instructors are responsible for those changes. This generalization also holds true across environments. When teachers, families, and community members notice that students' need for support is reduced, and that students have more opportunities available to them, accountability is obvious. Finally, when educators review long-term information on graduates that indicate training, employment, and independent living skills (1 to 5 years after completing school), they see information that indicates whether the school program has created positive, concrete results.

Conclusion

Assessing student progress and making instructional changes represents a very large portion of educational practices today. Basic knowledge of assessment types and of the use of evaluation tools to gather concise information evolves through much effort on the part of teachers and administrators. Getting started and using a systematic approach to overall assessment allows teachers' proficiency to grow and gives them the information they need to judge their instruction. By combining student and family desires, community input, administrative knowledge, and teacher experience, a school system can create a process to constantly evaluate and improve the districtwide use of CBI. State level changes continue to challenge schools, as do ever-present fiscal issues. Formal state assessments, alternative state assessments, and long-range outcomes all indicate accountability of instruction. A commitment to ongoing evaluation for the purpose of improving instruction and student opportunities indicates a dedication to best practices and ultimately translates to student independence in society.

Forms Related to Chapter 6—Appendix E

    Appendix E1 Checklist

    Appendix E2 Data Recording Sheets

    Appendix E3 Sample Rubrics

    Appendix E4 Performance Graphs

Points to Ponder

1. When is it beneficial to use commercial data collection materials, and when is it most appropriate for teachers to construct their own record sheets?

2. How can subjective assessment be made fair, consistent, and reliable?

3. Consider all of the tasks that should be assessed on an ongoing basis. Do some forms of assessment appear more appropriate for CBI than others?

4. What is the most efficient way to correlate daily activities with assessment to evaluate IEP objectives? How does a teacher begin with a simple process of assessment and move toward developing formats for all areas of instructions?

5. What role does technology play in the selection or development of assessment tools?

6. What form of assessment is valued in the local district? How are teachers trained to be consistent in evaluating students?

7. What methods exist to show accountability beyond statewide assessments and alternative assessments?

Suggested Reading

Clark G.M., Patton, J.R., & Moulton, L.R. (2000). *Informal assessments for transition planning*. Austin, TX: Pro-Ed.

McLoughlin, J.A., & Lewis, R.B. (2001). *Assessing students with special needs* (5th ed.). Upper Saddle River, NJ: Merrill/Prentice Hall.

Sitlington, P.L., Clark, G.M., & Kolstoe, O.P. (2000). *Transition education and services for adolescents with disabilities* (3rd. ed.). Boston: Allyn & Bacon.

Stiggins, R.J. (1997). *Student-centered classroom assessment* (2nd ed.) Upper Saddle River, NJ: Merrill/Prentice Hall.

Venn, J.J. (2000). *Assessing students with special needs* (2nd ed.). Upper Saddle River, NJ: Merrill/Prentice Hall.

Chapter 7

Maintaining and Generalizing Community Skills

> **In this chapter . . .**
>
> ◆ **What is meant by maintenance and generalization?**
>
> ◆ **What strategies create maintenance and generalization of skills?**
>
> ◆ **How are maintenance and generalization judged effective?**

What Is Meant by Maintenance and Generalization?

When an individual repeatedly performs a task in a variety of settings, teachers and families gain confidence that the student can function independently. Independence relies on the student's abilities to maintain skills over time and generalize those skills wherever they go. Maintenance and generalization may occur spontaneously, but assuring that skills and behaviors proceed—after formal instruction ends—takes planned, deliberate attention. If students received skill instruction that included repeated practice and promoted independence, then students should find it relatively easy to maintain and generalize those skills. To ensure that students constantly build on their acquired skills, retain those skills, and apply the skills to new situations, teachers should include maintenance and generalization activities into everyday routines. In the general curriculum, this may occur through review sessions or overlap of basic content and opportunity. For students with support needs, deliberate attempts to reinforce maintenance and generalization should be very structured. The discussion in this chapter is designed to increase these skills in all students but particularly in students who require support.

Maintenance

When students learn skills and behaviors, they must repeat them with accuracy over many trials. Students must also retrieve and utilize the skills whenever needed. Maintenance of acquired skills represents the continuation of competence over time. With many skills this occurs easily, for instance, the use of money. Although the items or services purchased may differ, basically the handling, budgeting, and use of money remains constant. Some skills, such as resetting an alarm clock to accommodate changes in schedules or occasions when the electricity fails, occur so rarely that more intentional intervention is needed. A correlation exists between maintaining and generalizing skills.

Generalization

The transfer of mastered skills to settings beyond the initial learning environment denotes generalization. In the broadest sense of transition planning, generalization represents the ultimate outcome of community skills. Generalization requires that students perform effectively, regardless of the setting, materials, or individuals accompanying them. Not only will students perform similar skills in similar locations, students will combine skills and select appropriate behaviors in complex situations. The use of computers provides an excellent example. Most software programs have some things in common and others that differ. Students who demonstrate efficient use of some forms of technology seem to be able to generalize those skills to other types of computer-based products.

What Strategies Create Maintenance and Generalization of Skills?

Creating maintenance and generalization includes all stakeholders. Teachers design CBI strategies to maintain and generalize skills. The educational process emphasizes the spiral effect of instruction, meaning that skills are constantly repeated, adding higher-level tasks and refining learned skills. Over time, some skills are maintained and generalized into new settings. However, human resources and educational budgets do not always allow for a thorough, systematic approach to generalization. Therefore, planning creative integration of maintenance and generalization activities becomes part of the overall teaching and learning process.

Skills that are generalizable are evident in all aspects of education and transition planning. Teachers work on these skills through academics, personal management, and independent living skills. Over the last two decades, James Greenan (1999) has researched and validated a list of generalizable skills through vocational education programs. He has verified his work with students with limited support needs as well as sensory impairments. Greenan included generalizable skills in mathematical skills, communication skills, interpersonal relation skills, and reasoning skills. He also compared student self-ratings with teacher ratings. Teachers may consider Greenan's work when examining CBI skills that must be maintained and generalized.

In the course of a day, everyone has opportunities to frequently and naturally generalize what they have learned in instructional settings. In addition, skills used in work settings transfer to other work and nonwork environments. Furthermore, including maintenance and generalization activities into a family's normal routine offers a much broader arena in which to practice skills than is available at school or in a work setting. With a structured school plan, organized work training program, ongoing home-school communication, and collaboration, the continuity and extension of community skills will naturally progress into family, work, and community life.

Planning for Maintenance Within the Structured Program

The individual student, and the opportunity to repeat a skill frequently, affect a student's ability to maintain learned skills over an extended period of time. With many community skills, it will be easy to repeat the skills so often that a planned time schedule is not necessary. Examples include activities such as following safety directions, asking for assistance, reading aisle markers, using public restrooms, or using coin-operated machines. Other skills, such as making reservations or ordering items from a catalog, occur so sporadically that, without a concentrated effort, the skills would be lost between opportunities. Inconsistent or infrequent skill opportunities require a maintenance schedule.

The Maintenance Schedule

Before creating a schedule, teachers should look at previously collected data. Careful records help the teacher create a reasonable pace of instruction. Likewise, prompts may be faded at a rate that ensures success. For example, if a student needs constant prompting, daily, for two weeks, to perform a task, a very slow deliberate schedule with gradual fading of prompts should occur. The maintenance schedule would use a cue hierarchy of verbal prompts and fade the frequency of prompts over time. As time between prompts increases, the teacher only provides assistive prompts on request. Very consistent prompts provide a bridge between the amount of help needed and total independence. In addition, the student learns the prompts and begins to self-prompt when needed.

On the other hand, if the student acquired a skill in a short period of time using minimal prompts, the teacher could use a rapid maintenance schedule. During instruction, the teacher establishes an environment that requires the use of the skill over a much longer interval, checking just to determine that the student can still perform the skill independently. The teacher may also have the student teach the skill to another student, or use the student to demonstrate the procedure. All of these activities reinforce the student's accomplishments and serve to encourage independence. Only if there is a change in performance would immediate reteaching or more frequent maintenance scheduling occur. For the most part, students recognize the activities in which they excel and they show pride in their independence.

In the case of students with extensive or pervasive support needs, the family is an essential component. If the skill represents a behavior that the family requested, the opportunity for repeated practice would be greater at home. An example of such a skill might be cleaning a pet cage. Performing the task at home becomes part of the maintenance schedule. Teacher-parent discussions determine how frequently the skills are needed. Teachers then suggest that the family allow the student to do the task independently as soon as he or she is capable. The family demonstrates that they expect the student to do the skill and gives the student enough time to complete the task. Families provide natural prompts, such as siblings or neighbors and the exact materials used, to complete the task. By receiving support for skill maintenance, families' participation with extended skills naturally increases.

As the teacher gains knowledge of the rate of acquisition for each student, the development of the need for a maintenance schedule becomes more apparent. Developing a few generic timelines will help with the maintenance of many different skills. Observation, documentation, and reflection on the data take the place of remembering minute details. Individuals who are present when the student uses the skill (peers or family members) influence the natural environment and support the successful occurrence of the skill over time. The same process occurs within the community when students interact with people they do not know. In cases outside of the classroom, the various stakeholders promote maintenance activities naturally, without forethought (see Appendix F1).

Planning for Generalization Within the Structured Program

Many factors limit the number of locations in which CBI can occur during school-time instruction. Time, distance from school, and the cost of transportation all influence the number of locations used to practice skills. By presenting a systematic approach to follow-up activities, students experience an expanded number of community settings. Performing the task across settings, varying materials, and changing support personnel, gives the student increased generalization opportunities. Enlisting help from families, administrators, and community members provides students with the opportunity to perform mastered skills in a variety of situations.

Accomplishing Generalization

Consistency helps students gain skills, repetition helps them maintain skills, and variety helps students generalize skills. Breaking down every possible situation into minute parts is impossible. Teachers cannot anticipate every nuance of life. Thinking in general terms, over a period of time, adds realistic expectations to instruction. For example, families of students with pervasive support needs want their family member to have as much independence as possible.

Helping students become independent by learning to generalize the skill it takes to open a door may not be as simple as it sounds. For example, the common doorknob has many shapes and sizes. Home and classroom doors have round doorknobs that rotate with wrist action. The inside of the same door may have a handle that is pushed down to activate. To enter the restroom, a user simply pushes the door inward. Once inside the restroom, there is a small lever the user must lift and pull to get into the stall. To leave the school building, students may have to push a bar handle. The outside door of the library or grocery store works automatically and is activated by stepping on a black pad. Therefore, learning to open a door requires a great deal of discrimination. If a student has significant needs, getting to the other side of a door is not easy. Through repeated use of many types of doors, the student develops a repertoire of skills and generalizes that skill. In the community, the generalization of many of the skills students frequently need becomes an essential part of CBI. By varying the materials, the setting, and the individuals involved, students gain experience that will lead to generalization of isolated skills and, ultimately, to greater independence.

Generalization Across Settings

To prove students have mastered skills, they can perform those skills in a variety of settings. Because each setting requires slightly different behaviors, students use problem-solving abilities to apply what they know from one setting to perform a similar task in another setting. By learning a process, rather than the details of specific locations, students demonstrate greater success than they would by practicing the skill in the same location. Opportunities in a small town may be limited to a few key places. Teachers need to plan early for experiences in locations farther from school, ideally before requesting funds. With time and practice, the student with support needs recognizes similarities and differences in settings and can draw on past experience for present performance.

Generalization Using Different Materials or Methods

As in the doorknob example, common materials vary from place to place. Subtle differences exist in washing machines at laundromats or in the operation of vending machines. Checkout counters vary in number from several in a supermarket to just one in a convenience store, but they all have a cashier and a counter on which to place items. Significant differences exist in how we pay for food between a full service restaurant, a buffet, and a fast food chain. However, all fast food restaurants have a basic counter to order food, a waiting line, and one contact person who is the waiter and the cashier. The anticipation of receiving a good lunch creates the motivation for most students to adapt to the methods used in any given location. Consequently, students do not seem to have difficulty transferring ordering skills between different fast food restaurants. To vary materials, teachers can arrange many types of similar experiences within a small geographic area. Both minor and significant changes in materials or methods enrich the student's ability to apply basic knowledge to handling materials or the methods of performing the desired tasks.

Generalization With a Variety of Support Personnel

The last step in generalizing skills calls for a variety of individuals to work with the student. The use of several support personnel adds depth to students' skills. Different individuals such as specialists, paraeducators, community workers, parents, or peer assistants allow the student to receive instructions in many different ways. When working with different individuals, the goal changes to interdependence, rather than independence, and the ability to effectively communicate becomes paramount. If students cannot locate toothpaste, they should ask the clerk for assistance. The clerk, not knowing how the teacher gave directions, uses very different phrases to communicate information. The teacher could instruct students to locate an item by telling them to look up and use the aisle markers. The clerk may say, "over in aisle five." A parent might say, "I just look for the toothbrush stand; the toothpaste is near that." Following several different sets of instructions gives students a broad array of possible solutions, when they must solve situations without assistance. At this point of learning, intentional variety increases the likelihood that the student can generalize learned skills in new locations.

The Generalization Plan

The generalization plan becomes a fundamental part of any instructional strategy. As a fluid and dynamic procedure, the addition of environments and the use of ongoing adjustments reflect the spiral effect of transferring skills to new settings. The basic generalization plan can be used across ages and student ability levels. The list of competencies designed by parents and teachers, and the list of steps to achieve those competencies, form an outline for the instructional sequence. Watching the student progress through the activities needed to achieve one set of community skills will make it easier to recognize the pattern to use when learning another set of community skills. A generalization matrix could take two formats. One would be the skill-level approach of using a skill in several locations. The location approach uses one location and practices many skills in that location. The choice of approach depends on the specific skill, number of settings available, and teacher preference.

Students benefit from both approaches. The skill level approach works well in the lower grades and with entry-level or prerequisite skills. Where there are more opportunities to implement acquired skills, such as in middle and high school programs, the location approach adds continuity and complexity to the generalization of skills. Teachers may also choose to create an individual or classroom generalization plan. Creating a usable format may take several trials. The skill and performance level will change accordingly, but the locations may be consistent based on the specific attributes of a setting. When the local information and family components are added, the process works well for most students (see Appendix F2).

Communicating Activities, Involving Families, and Eliciting Support

Teachers can use several formal and informal methods to communicate the overall plan for maintenance and generalization to families. Formal methods occur through open houses, teacher conferences, multidisciplinary evaluations, IEP development conferences, and progress reports. Informal communications take place during activities such as volunteer days, newsletters, memorandums, and student feedback forms. Each one of these events represents opportunities to share information about the use of CBI and encourage outside activities that support maintenance and generalization skills. Time spent on the creation of communication modes saves hours of repeating the information over the phone or through handwritten notes. Figure 7-1 includes a few of the most common forms of communication.

How Are Maintenance and Generalization Judged Effective?

When students display independence and interdependence over time, in many environments, teachers can see the effectiveness of maintenance and generalization instruction. Much of the assessment discussion of Chapter 6 applies to the long-term retention of skills. By working maintenance and generalization goals into the initial and ongoing assessment plans, teachers develop a sequence and timetable to revisit skills on a regular, but increasingly less frequent, basis. This ensures that retention and usefulness of skills has occurred. Helping students master functional, frequently used skills is a major focus of the CBI program. Students have natural opportunities to continually generalize skills. In those cases, less intentional planning for maintenance and generalization is needed. If regression of skills occurs, teachers return to the systematic maintenance and generalization schedule.

Newsletters	The monthly newsletter provides a friendly, informative avenue to let caregivers know what is happening in school. It includes suggestions for creative follow-through activities that practice, reinforce, maintain, and generalize skills. Naturally, the setting, materials, and individuals differ from the initial instruction, thus creating opportunities to transfer learned skills.
Questionnaires	Teachers may use questionnaires at the beginning of each unit as a way to share information. Questionnaires communicate the areas of emphasis and personalize the activities used during instruction. When using questionnaires, teachers should allow for open-ended responses. Families will recognize that their input is valued.
Charts	Charts are simple and informative. They do not allow for two-way communication in the way that questionnaires do, but they do share important information that promotes maintaining and generalizing skills.
Memos	Teacher-created memos provide a simple home-school communication. By creating a consistent format, a teacher saves time writing repetitive information, yet can easily personalize the content of the memo for the individual student.
Volunteers	A few hours spent on basic training keeps all interested adults informed and aware of student goals, progress, and further needs. Initial time used to explain how students maintain and generalize skills helps volunteers realize the importance of their involvement in helping students extend acquired skills. In addition, recognizing and publicly stating the school's appreciation of volunteers emphasizes how important their contribution is to students, families, and teachers (see Appendix F3).

Figure 7-1   Common Forms of Communication

Assessing Maintenance Schedules and Generalization Plans

Assessing for maintenance and generalization follows the same process as the pre- and post-assessment stated in the assessment plan. As mentioned in Chapter 6, documentation of student progress demonstrates the accountability of the instructional methods. Student data must include information about skill retention. As with overall assessment, charting, graphing, or any quick and easy format can be productive when deciding if a student maintained a skill over time or can use the skill in other settings. The easiest way to check maintenance is to keep a cumulative record of student progress during instruction. Then teachers can revisit the same evaluation process at a later time. To check generalization, the same evaluation forms used during instruction can be taken into never-visited locations and used in the same manner. Additional columns or a second page added to the original assessment plan allows space to state reassessment dates and outcomes. Teachers will recapture the initial time spent in developing usable maintenance schedules, generalization plans and recording devices by making them applicable to all settings. The overall assessment of maintenance and generalization skills ultimately helps the teacher review student performance and planning for future instruction. As with all types of assessment, most secondary students can be made responsible for their own documentation. They will gain insight into their personal learning styles in the process of recording and interpreting the data. When students record their own data, they monitor their own progress and give teachers the information to make informed instructional decisions.

Moving to the Next Step

In some cases "ready" means "never." Some individuals who have difficulties with acquisition, maintenance, and generalization never seem to get beyond the initial training because the instructor is not convinced that they have mastered the prerequisite skills. The theory behind a systematic approach suggests that students get a hierarchy of skills and progress in a deliberate manner to acquire those skills. Teachers have to give students a chance to make mistakes. If students did not learn to write until they perfected their spelling and grammar, they might never get there. Teachers even encourage inventive spelling in the primary years. The same philosophy can be applied to learning community skills. Teachers concentrate on specific skills in specific settings, but by getting the whole picture and doing the entire task, students are more likely to realize the importance of what occurs in the progression of skills leading to a desired outcome. Students may even develop their own compensatory skills to complete a desirable task. Therefore, teachers' flexibility and informed decision-making during instruction is an essential component of the overall acquisition, maintenance, and generalization of skills.

Even in the most ideal programs, a large amount of time is spent in the classroom. Typically, reteaching isolated steps occurs offsite. Teachers may have students make one-task trips throughout the school building to gain repeated practice. For example, if a lesson objective is for students to open doors, teachers can create an in-school or out-of-school route that contains 15 doors to allow students to experience the array of common doorknobs. When the overall goal is for students to participate in a shopping trip to the local mall, they will have opportunities to practice and generalize the door-opening objective at the mall. Teachers should not delay motivating activities, such as a trip to the mall, for the mundane tasks of opening doors. However, teachers should offer methods for students to obtain assistance. Then, when a difficult door appears, students have a strategy to get it open by asking for help. Setting the priority of the objectives and the overall maintenance and generalization schedule alleviates many of the challenges that occur in the community.

Conclusion

The whole purpose of CBI is to ensure that students can retain skills over time and can use them appropriately in a variety of settings. A deliberate attempt to include maintenance and generalization skills and assessment into the instructional cycle ensures the ultimate goal of community learning. As students progress, natural repetition of mastered skills creates the best opportunity to use previously learned skills. For skills that do not occur on a frequent basis, planning schedules that recheck skills over time represents the best way to guarantee retention.

Forms Related to Chapter 7—Appendix F

Appendix F1 Maintenance Schedules

Appendix F2 Generalization Schedules

Appendix F3 Communication to Gain Support

Points to Ponder

1. Think about how often the average person uses an automated banking machine. Why is it so much easier to withdraw money than deposit money? How can knowledge of making a withdrawal be applied to making a deposit through an automated banking machine?

2. How do you vote? Would a student who has been taught to vote in one state have the ability to apply that in a neighboring state? Make a list of activities that have a basic process, yet require many different applications. What community skills must be frequently applied to ensure students can complete this task in a variety of ways?

3. How can the teacher enlist families to provide support that will systematically assist students with the maintenance and generalization of acquired CBI skills?

References

Greenan, J.P. (1999). Relationship between self-rating by sensory impaired students and teachers' ratings of generalizable skills. *Journal of Visual Impairment and Blindness, 99*, 716-728.

Suggested Reading

Sitlington, P.L., Clark, G.M., & Kolstoe, O.P. (2000). *Transition education and services for adolescents with disabilities* (3rd. ed.). Boston: Allyn & Bacon.

Westling, D.L., & Fox, L. (2000). *Teaching students with severe disabilities* (2nd ed.). Upper Saddle River, NJ: Merrill/Prentice Hall.

Chapter 8

The Dynamics of Community-Based Instruction

In this chapter . . .

◆ **How are schools changing?**

◆ **How are changes in schools influencing the use of CBI?**

How are Schools Changing?

Change is not new to any of the entities that affect students and teachers today. What seems different in schools, communities, and society is the pace of change and the reliance on highly sophisticated technology. In the past, noticeable change was brought about by innovation. Today's schools change because of new technology and changes in demographics, families, and safety issues. Children that used to be protected and sheltered from adult matters often have pertinent information before their parents. These experiences emphasize how much school has changed in the last several decades.

Schools change to meet the times and the needs of students and society. They have gone from very structured and domineering settings to learning communities and cooperative partnerships. Inclusive practices are commonplace. Worldwide information can be accessed by the classroom computer. Scheduling has gone from traditional time blocks to block scheduling. Vocational education, once the primary option for students not interested in academic careers, utilizes some of the most expensive and technical equipment owned by school systems. General curricular programming, team arrangements, and integration of specialized classrooms throughout the school have replaced many of the segregated special education programs. Transition planning and school-to-work projects that serve all students have superseded the work-study programs designed to combine education and employment with the hopes that students would remain in the educational system until graduation. There is no end to the significant and well-intended changes in schools.

How Are Changes in Schools Influencing the Use of CBI?

Community-based instruction evolved over the years and changed focus in keeping with the educational climate. The use of CBI progressed from short walking trips for brief observational outings to the very sophisticated practice of advanced students attending enrichment activities that cannot be duplicated in school. The most recent change has been the implementation of standards-based curriculum and assessment. This has made teachers pay close attention to student performance and take more ownership of the students' progress in all curricular areas. All students participate in community activities to the extent necessary to learn content outlined by standards. The proportion of the curriculum spent outside of school is directly related to students' needs. For some students, most community skills are learned through family outings in the early years, during off-school times, and after graduation. As mentioned several times throughout this book, students' skill acquisition will likely depend on a school program that offers direct instruction in the community as part of the curriculum.

The need for highly effective instruction has never been more important. The use of every available resource inside and outside of school provides the enhanced relationships schools need within the communities they serve. In addition, the inclusion of community-referenced learning in standards and accountability initiatives greatly increases the number of students participating in CBI and significantly expands the environments needed to meet the needs of all students. Practices that were initially designed to serve a small portion of the school population that needs extensive support now include strategies that support all students. Advanced students receive enriched experiences, typical students expand their career options, and students with pervasive support needs practice functional skills that allow them to participate in the same adult activities as the general public.

This guidebook was conceived to support the educational process for both the general curriculum and specialized programs. They are similar in that:

- Educational teams recognize that the most effective instruction to meet students' needs may be in the ecological setting pertinent to that task.

- Community-based instruction is systematic, requires intense planning, and involves the commitment of all stakeholders—families, school professionals, community members, local businesses, and industries.

- Assessment is the key to making informed decisions about needs, strategies, and performance.

- Logistical challenges must be handled by a team of professionals with the goals of serving students in the best possible manner.

- There is no "one-size-fits-all" program in education. The ideas contained in this guide must be custom designed to meet the needs, opportunities, and resources of the local district.

Teams that determine CBI need to evaluate the methods now used, assess resources and possibilities, and begin in a systematic manner with small, manageable increments. Structure, creativity, and persistence will reward efforts through long-term accomplishments. Instruction in the community does not occur without challenges. Perhaps the biggest challenge teachers face is to provide a comprehensive program for a very diverse group of students and to find the preparation time to develop beneficial instruction for all students they serve, in all settings they utilize. CBI is a practical and realistic way to provide today's students with the skills they need to face their world beyond the school building.

Appendix A—Forms

LCCE Competencies

Curriculum Area	Competency	Subcompetency: The student will be able to:	
DAILY LIVING SKILLS	1. Managing Personal Finances	1. Count money & make correct change	2. Make responsible expenditures
	2. Selecting & Managing a Household	7. Maintain home exterior/interior	8. Use basic appliances and tools
	3. Caring for Personal Needs	12. Demonstrate knowledge of physical fitness, nutrition, & weight	13. Exhibit proper grooming & hygiene
	4. Raising Children & Meeting Marriage Responsibilities	17. Demonstrate physical care for raising children	18. Know psychological aspects of raising children
	5. Buying, Preparing, & Consuming Food	20. Purchase food	21. Clean food preparation areas
	6. Buying & Caring for Clothing	26. Wash/clean clothing	27. Purchase clothing
	7. Exhibiting Responsible Citizenship	29. Demonstrate knowledge of civil rights & responsibilities	30. Know nature of local, state, & federal governments
	8. Utilizing Recreational Facilities & Engaging in Leisure	33. Demonstrate knowledge of available community resources	34. Choose & plan activities
	9. Getting Around the Community	38. Demonstrate knowledge of traffic rules & safety	39. Demonstrate knowledge & use of various means of transportation
PERSONAL-SOCIAL SKILLS	10. Achieving Self-Awareness	42. Identify physical & psychological needs	43. Identify interests & abilities
	11. Acquiring Self-Confidence	46. Express feelings of self-worth	47. Describe others' perception of self
	12. Achieving Socially Responsible Behavior	51. Develop respect for the rights & properties of others	52. Recognize authority & follow instructions
	13. Maintaining Good Interpersonal Skills	56. Demonstrate listening & responding skills	57. Establish & maintain close relationships
	14. Achieving Independence	59. Strive toward self-actualization	60. Demonstrate self-organization
	15. Making Adequate Decisions	62. Locate & utilize sources of assistance	63. Anticipate consequences
	16. Communicating with Others	67. Recognize & respond to emergency situations	68. Communicate with understanding
OCCUPATIONAL GUIDANCE AND PREPARATION	17. Knowing & Exploring Occupational Possibilities	70. Identify remunerative aspects of work	71. Locate sources of occupational & training information
	18. Selecting & Planning Occupational Choices	76. Make realistic occupational choices	77. Identify requirements of appropriate & available jobs
	19. Exhibiting Appropriate Work Habits & Behavior	81. Follow directions & observe regulations	82. Recognize importance of attendance & punctuality
	20. Seeking, Securing, & Maintaining Employment	88. Search for a job	89. Apply for a job
	21. Exhibiting Sufficient Physical-Manual Skills	94. Demonstrate stamina & endurance	95. Demonstrate satisfactory balance & coordination
	22. Obtaining Specific Occupational Skills		

LCCE Competencies (continued)

3. Keep basic financial records	4. Calculate & pay taxes	5. Use credit responsibly	6. Use banking services	
9. Select adequate housing	10. Set up household	11. Maintain home grounds		
14. Dress appropriately	15. Demonstrate knowledge of common illness, prevention & treatment	16. Practice personal safety		
19. Demonstrate marriage responsibilities				
22. Store food	23. Prepare meals	24. Demonstrate appropriate eating habits	25. Plan/eat balanced meals	
28. Iron, mend, & store clothing				
31. Demonstrate knowledge of the law & ability to follow the law	32. Demonstrate knowledge of citizen rights & responsibilities			
35. Demonstrate knowledge of the value of recreation	36. Engage in group & individual activities	37. Plan vacation time		
40. Find way around the community	41. Drive a car			
44. Identify emotions	45. Demonstrate knowledge of physical self			
48. Accept & give praise	49. Accept & give criticism	50. Develop confidence in oneself		
53. Demonstrate appropriate behavior in public areas	54. Know important character traits	55. Recognize personal roles		
58. Make & maintain friendships				
61. Demonstrate awareness of how one's behavior affects others				
64. Develop & evaluate alternatives	65. Recognize nature of a problem	66. Develop goal-seeking behavior		
69. Know subtleties of communication				
72. Identify personal values met through work	73. Identify societal values met through work	74. Classify jobs into occupational categories	75. Investigate local occupational & training opportunities	
78. Identify occupational aptitudes	79. Identify major occupational interests	80. Identify major occupational needs		
83. Recognize importance of supervision	84. Demonstrate knowledge of occupational safety	85. Work with others	86. Meet demands for quality work	87. Work at a satisfactory rate
90. Interview for a job	91. Know how to maintain postschool occupational adjustment	92. Demonstrate knowledge of competitive standards	93. Know how to adjust to changes in employment	
96. Demonstrate manual dexterity	97. Demonstrate sensory discrimination			
There are no specific subcompetencies, as they depend on skill being taught.				

Appendix B—Forms

B1—Pre-Inventory Notice

Dear Students, Parents, and Guardians,

Coming soon. Watch for three important inventories!

In the next few days an important set of surveys will be sent home. The purpose of these is to gather information prior to discussing transition outcomes for your young adult. You will receive three inventories on three different days. Each inventory offers information to help us plan interaction in the community and prepare for transition meetings. The inventories are as follows:

Inventory 1 - Interests
> This will be completed by the student. You may assist, but be sure that the responses are "their" words.

Inventory 2 - Preferences
> These will be completed by (a) the student and (b) the family. For this inventory the school would like to have input from both the student and the family as to their desires for goals and program concentration prior to the student's graduation.

Inventory 3 - Needs
> These will be completed by (a) the student, (b) the family, and (c) the teacher. We will all express our feelings about goals that need to be addressed prior to graduation.

Your response is essential. As you receive the inventories, please take time to thoroughly complete each item and return it to school. A complete school program and transition into adult life begin with a clear understanding of what the student and family want for the future.

Sincerely,

Mrs. McCall

Where we are going? What are we doing?
Make sure you mark these dates on your calendar -Thanks!

APRIL HAPPENINGS:

April 12 - P.O.

April 13 - NO SCHOOL - Holiday

April 20 - Breakfast at Eat & Park & Warwick Theater

April 24 - EARLY DISMISSAL

April 27 - Swimming at the Rec. $2

JUNE HAPPENINGS:

June 1 - Picnic with H.S.

June 4 - Lunch at Hoss's

June 5 - Last day of school (There will be 2 Early Dismissals and I will let you know closer to the time)

MAY HAPPENINGS:

May 4 - Warwick Theater

May 9- Baseball Game & Family Picnic

May 11- Challenge Day - Cedar Crest H.S.

May 14 - Challenge Day Raindate

May 18 - Bowling at Dutch Lanes

May 22 - Central Market & McDonalds

May 25 - Swimming at the REC - $2

May 28 - NO SCHOOL - HOLIDAY

B3—A Page in a Teacher-Made Parent Handbook

COMMUNITY BASED INSTRUCTION

In order for any individual to live successfully in the community, he or she must have the skills to use resources such as stores, theaters, mass transit systems, and banks. This ability to use community resources clearly affects the quality of life for the individual with developmental disabilities. It also affects perceptions of other community members about the competence of people with disabilities.

No one learns to participate successfully in the community without direct training. For most of us, this training is done informally by our families and is expanded upon in our adult lives through interactions with peers. Unfortunately, most students with developmental disabilities require more formal training to develop these competencies. Therefore, our program must be structured so that students are provided regular opportunities to receive instruction in community settings on personal management and leisure activities that will improve their competence in the community in which they live (p.10).

This is the goal of our program—to make the student as independent as possible in the community by mixing in academics, discussions, role-playing, classroom activities, and actual trips into the community 1-2 times a week.

Areas covered are:

Pedestrian/Community Safety, Community Social Skills, Grocery Shopping, Restaurant, Post Office, Rec. Center and Public Busing Skills

Created with information from:

McDonnell, J., Wilcox, B., & Hardman, M.L. (1991). *Secondary programs for students with developmental disabilities.* Boston: Allyn & Bacon

Community-Based Instruction

TRAVEL PERMISSION SLIP

Dear Parents/Guardians,

During the school year, your son/daughter will be participating in Community Trips. The purpose of these trips is to help the students perform skills, learned in the classroom, out in other settings.

In order for your son/daughter to participate in the community trips like going out to eat, grocery shopping, post office trips and snacks in (Anytown), we must have your written permission below. My assistant, other adults who may be helping in the class, and I supervise these trips closely.

Transportation will include school vans and public bus. Other trips will consist of walking downtown. Occasionally, we may need to use our cars.

<u>Please sign below and return this slip on the first day of school so that your son/daughter can participate. We will be going out into the community the first week.</u>

Please do not hesitate to call me here at Anytown Middle School, before or after school at <u>(555-2222)</u> if you have any questions/concerns about any of our trips. We are looking forward to another productive year in the community.

Sincerely,
(teacher's name)

_____ has permission to participate in the community trips as part of their instruction this year.

_____   _____
Parent/Guardian Signature   Date

<u>We must have this permission slip in hand before your son/daughter may go out on community trips.</u>

B5—Excerpts of Teacher-Made Ecological Inventories
Each inventory would have student, family, and teacher forms.
Inventory 1 - Interests

Name _____   Date _____

1. What are your favorite school subjects?

   _____
   _____
   _____

2. What kind of job do you think you want to do?

   _____
   _____
   _____

3. What is your favorite recreational activity?

   _____
   _____
   _____

4. With whom do you like to spend your time, for example, alone, with family, with friends?

   _____
   _____
   _____

5. Where would you like to live as an adult?

   _____
   _____
   _____

6. What are your goals after graduation?

   _____
   _____
   _____

7. If you could have one wish, what would you wish?

   _____
   _____
   _____

B5—Excerpts of Teacher-Made Ecological Inventories (continued)
Inventory 2 - Preferences—Parent/Guardian/Caretaker Form

Student Name _____

Form completed by_____ Date _____

1. Do you envision _____living independently upon graduation?

   a. Totally independent
   b. Independent with family support
   c. Shared living with another person
   d. Supervised living with another person

2. Does _____have family responsibility?

   a. Many responsibilities.
   b. Minimal responsibility.
   c. No chores or responsibility
   d. Totally dependent

3. Do you prefer that _____ . . .?

   a. Take full responsibility for her or his daily living tasks
   b. Receive minimal supervision for daily living tasks
   c. Receive concentrated supervision for daily living tasks
   d. Receive total support for daily living tasks

4. Where would you like _____to work?

   a. In a competitive job in the community
   b. In a supported environment
   c. With family members
   d. We prefer _____does not seek employment

5. Who will provide transportation for _____to get to work?

   a. The family
   b. Public transportation
   c. Co-workers
   d. Agency-provided vehicle

6. Would you like _____to participate in . . .?

   a. Leisure activities in the community at large
   b. Integrated leisure activities
   c. Family leisure activities
   d. Leisure activities with individuals with support needs

B5—Excerpts of Teacher-made Ecological Inventories (continued)
Inventory 3 - Needs—Teacher Form

Student Name _____

Form completed by_____ Date_____

	Displays Skills	Goal Needed
Job Skills		
1. Can complete an application.	_____	_____
2. Demonstrates appropriate interview skills.	_____	_____
3. Demonstrates strength and endurance.	_____	_____
4. Expresses the type of work he or she likes.	_____	_____
Living Skills		
1. Displays proper hygiene.	_____	_____
2. Cares for clothing and possessions.	_____	_____
3. Manages personal items in a neat fashion.	_____	_____
4. Can budget money and make purchases.	_____	_____
Leisure Skills		
1. Expresses the type of activities he/she likes.	_____	_____
2. Participates appropriately in leisure activities.	_____	_____
3. Arranges leisure activities independently.	_____	_____

Clark, G.M, Patton, J.R., & Moulton, L.R. (2000). *Informal assessments for transition planning.* Austin, TX: Pro-Ed.

Hutchins, M.P., & Renzaglia, A. (1998). Interviewing families for effective transition to employment. *Teaching Exceptional Children, 30*(4), 73.

Tolls for Transition. (1991). Circle Pines, MN: American Guidance Service.

B6—SAMPLE—District Permission Form

Community-Based Instruction
Permission and Transportation Request Form

Teacher: _____ Date of Request: _____

Class Location: _____ Classroom Phone: _____

Date of CBI Trip:

_____

Destination:

_____

Leave School At: _____ Return To School At: _____

Objectives for the Trip:

_____

_____

_____

_____

Relationship to the Curriculum:

_____

_____

_____

_____

Safety Plan:

_____

_____

_____

❑ **Transportation Needs To Be Arranged**

Number Of Students: _____ Number Of Adults: _____

Special Considerations: (Wheelchair Vans)_____

❑ **No Transportation Required**

    Walk ❑   Personal Auto ❑   Other ❑

Teacher Signature: _____

Administrator Signature: _____

Office Use Only

Request ❑ Approved   ❑ Denied

Transportation Coordinator Signature: _____

B7—Requesting Support

Anytown High School, Anytown, USA, September 4, 2000

Dear Organization President:

Anytown High School has a Life Management Class that spends some instructional time in the community to help students learn independent living skills. The attached brochure tells a little about the goals and procedures of the Community-based Instruction Program. As with many of the school programs, it is nice to have community organization support. Support for this program can come in many forms. Interested individuals can support the program by volunteering time in the classroom or at training sites. Financial contributions from the organization are also appreciated.

We invite you to schedule a time to come to school and see the program that has been developed to increase the independent living skills of our students. We are proud of the accomplishments the students have made and their ability to function in the community. Thank you for your consideration and interest in our school.

Sincerely,
Mr. Bob Smith, Teacher
Life Management Program

Anytown High School, Anytown, USA, September 4, 2000

Dear Local Business:

Anytown High School has a Life Management Class that spends some instructional time in the community, to help students learn independent living skills. The attached brochure tells a little about the goals and procedures of the Community-based Instruction Program. As with many of the school programs, it is nice to have support from community businesses. Support for this program can come in many forms. Sharing your place of business, considering working with our employee training program, and making financial contributions are all appreciated.

We invite you to schedule a time to come to school and see the program that has been developed to increase the independent living skills of our students. We are proud of the accomplishments the students have made and their ability to function in the community. Thank you for your consideration and interest in our school.

Sincerely,
Mr. Bob Smith, Teacher
Life Management Program

B8—General Lesson Plan Format

Lesson:	State the name of the lesson as it is listed in the overall unit.
Objectives:	State what the student will do as a result of the instruction. Objectives must be: Specific, Observable, Measurable. Criteria for acceptable response or action must be stated in terms so that not only the teacher can recognize the behavior but other observers as well could say, "Yes, the student performed this action."
Materials:	What will the teacher need to teach this lesson? Include all teacher and student materials needed. If commercial items, videos, or consumables are used, specify where the items can be obtained or include a reference.
Procedures:	In simple terms, the procedure is the teacher teaching and the student practicing the behaviors called for in the objectives. However, this is not a simple task. Each objective listed must be addressed. The teacher must explain, demonstrate, model, and guide the student about how to perform the task. In response, the teacher gives the student a time for structured (or guided) practice while the teacher is present to correct errors and repeat the instruction if needed. The student then demonstrates the task for the teacher or does several repetitions of the behavior. This is also where adaptations or prompts are stated and utilized to ensure student success with the behavior. Prior to leaving this portion of the lesson, the teacher conducts a brief check to determine if the student has understood instruction. When satisfied, the teacher provides a summary and closure.
Evaluation:	Finally, the teacher must determine and document if the student has mastered the skill identified in the objective. This may include interpretation of data collected during the lesson, a rubric evaluation, or artifact for a portfolio. Teacher reflection about the lesson is also documented.

B9—Sample Lesson Plans

Lesson:	Locating an item by brand, size, and type.
Objective:	The student will locate the correct item, brand, and size in the grocery store.
Materials:	Empty food containers, picture cards of grocery item, coupon type pictures, written cards (item name, brand name, size, and type), timer, tables, shelf units.
Procedures:	**Locating items:** 1. Put out several grocery items/picture item cards on the table and have the students practice locating items. 2. At the grocery store, have the students practice locating items using picture cards. **Locating brands:** 1. After students have learned what each of the items are, take two of the same kind of item and put them together 2. Discuss that these are the same kind of items but they are also different. 3. Ask: "Does anyone know what the differences are?" 4. If students do not know, discuss that they have different brand names. Discuss what a brand name is. 5. Have the students practice locating the brand name of items. 6. At the grocery store, have the students practice locating items using pictures or written cards. **Locating size:** 1. Put out the same item and brand name (i.e., Minute rice) but different sizes. 2. Describe sizes of items and where to find the size. 3. Have the students practice locating the size. 4. At the grocery store, have the students practice locating the sizes of items with written cards or use coupons.

B9—Sample Lesson Plans (continued)

Classroom: Activities	**1. Play games around these skills:** Collect as many empty grocery containers as you can and put them out on tables, or you can use coupon type pictures. a. Break into teams and have one student from each team collect as many of the same item in one minute (point for each correct item). b. Set up tables with categories of grocery items (i.e., household, breakfast items, dairy) Break into teams—teaming same-skill students against each other. Have the students find as many items using written cards (brand, size, and type) as they can in one minute (putting them into a box up front and getting a new card). Students with lower skills—use picture cards. Give points for each correct item collected. **2. Shopping Station:** a. Have the students match written cards with picture cards (pictures from coupons or store circulars). b. Set up store area in the back using shelf units. Put empty grocery containers on shelves in similar categories; have the students practice locating items using written/ picture cards. c. Have the students read prices on shelves by locating items in store area and reading the price to a teacher. d. Have students put shopping cards under different categories that you would find on an aisle sign. e. Have students put shopping cards under mini-aisle signs by reading aisle sign to locate where item would be found. f. Have students locate the aisle number by matching it to the shopping card (two ways—aisle numbers hanging from classroom ceiling or on a bulletin board display with pockets for cards).
Evaluation:	1. The teacher will assess what skills the student needs to work on through observation during classroom work. 2. In the grocery store, the teacher uses a 1-4 rubric scale (4-independent, 3-verbal assistance, 2-physical assistance, 1-total assistance) to determine what the student can transfer from the classroom to the store and what needs to still be addressed.

B10—Transition Site Survey

	Location 1	Location 2	Location 3
Name			
Manager			
Phone Number			
Address			
Hours			
Instruction			
Supports			
Special Features			
Other Information			

Note: The CBI coordinator or teacher can use this general information as a reminder of information to collect.

Adapted From: S.R. Lyon, Domaracki, G.A. Lyon, & S.G. Warsinske (1990). *Community membership. Preparation for integrated community living and employment: Curriculum and program development.* Harrisburg, PA: Pennsylvania Department of Education.

C2—Sample of Basic Skills (continued)

10. Functional Writing			
✓ Done	**Basic Skill**	**Locations to Practice**	**Strategies & Materials**
	Filling in simple applications		
	Filling in simple forms		
	Filling in bank book transactions		
	Writing simple letters		
11. Printing Skills			
	In neatness		
	In allotted space		
	On given line		
	Use of uppercase and lowercase letters		
LOCATIONS TO PRACTICE SKILLS—KEY			
	Post Office	PO	
	Banking	B	

C2—Sample of Basic Skills (continued)

Other Functional Skills		
12. Cooking Skills—Basic Skills	**Locations to Practice**	**Strategies & Materials**
Measuring cups—dry		
Measuring spoons—dry		
Measuring cups—liquid		
Measuring spoons—liquid		
Cutting		
Spreading		
Operating a microwave		
Operating a stove		
Operating an oven		
Pouring		
Mixing		
Scraping a bowl		
Setting a timer		
Cracking an egg		
13. Cooking Skills—Clean Up		
Wiping off ingredients before putting away		
Putting ingredients away in proper place		
Cleaning up cooking area—tables, stove, etc.		
Washing dishes & equipment		
Drying dishes & equipment		
Putting equipment away in proper place		
Wringing out rag and hanging it up properly to dry		
LOCATIONS TO PRACTICE SKILLS—KEY		
Grocery store	GS	
Restaurant	R	
Post Office	PO	
Bank	B	
Leisure location	L	

C2—Sample of Basic Skills (continued)

14. Health—Hygiene/Grooming	Locations to Practice	Strategies & Materials
Making sure clothes are adjusted properly after going to the bathroom. Putting on coat before a trip		
Wearing clothes appropriate for the weather—coat, gloves, hat		
Carrying items for weather—umbrella		
Washing hands at appropriate times (before and after eating, after going to the bathroom, sneezing/coughing)		
Blowing nose when runny		
Keeping hair neat after coming in from outside/before a trip		
Keeping face clean after snack/lunch/meal at a restaurant		
15. Health – Safety Skills		
Knife—cutting safely		
Microwave—what not to put in a microwave		
Stove—what not to do around a stove—fire		
Oven—what not to do around an oven—fire		
Electrical—appliances, fire		
General safety—water/spills		
Water safety—swimming		
Pedestrian—sidewalks/parking lot		
Transportation		
Grocery store—cart		
Restaurant—belongings out of the way of others		
Money—put in a safe place		
Belongings—put in safe place		

LOCATIONS TO PRACTICE SKILLS—KEY		
Grocery store	GS	
Restaurant	R	
Post Office	PO	
Bank	B	
Leisure location	L	

C2—Sample of Basic Skills (continued)

16. Social Skills—Following Directions		Locations to Practice	Strategies & Materials
	Following Routines— Remembering to take check when paying Waiting for change when paying		
	Following Verbal Directions— Waiting in line until called Locating items		
	Getting Out Materials Needed for an Activity— Making sure to have everything for a trip Having wallet ready when paying		
	Listening Skills		
	Carrying Out Task With Minimal Assistance— Waiting for change Locating an area		
	Carrying Out Tasks in a Required Amount of Time— Getting groceries in a short amount of time		
	Staying on Task		
17. Social Skills—Acting Appropriately			
	Acceptable Comments— Noises Imitating others		
	Acceptable Behaviors— No touching people/grocery item No hanging/hugging on strangers Inappropriate laughing Pestering Learning to wait patiently		
	Good Community Manners— Walk on one side of sidewalk Not blocking an entrance in/out of a building/aisles Moving when someone needs an item on a shelf		
LOCATIONS TO PRACTICE SKILLS—KEY			
	Grocery store	GS	
	Restaurant	R	
	Post Office	PO	
	Bank	B	
	Leisure location	L	

C2—Sample of Basic Skills (continued)

18. Social Skills—Communication Skills		Locations to Practice	Strategies & Materials
	Using an Appropriate Voice Volume— Asking for help/service/item Ordering a meal		
	Expressing Needs Appropriately— Asking for help Talking with cashier/waitress		
	No Tattling (minding own business)		
	No Interrupting		
	Acknowledging Others When Spoken To		
	Using Good Manners— Please, thank you, and excuse me		
	Using Good Eye Contact		
	Expressing Emotions Appropriately— Asking for help		
LOCATIONS TO PRACTICE SKILLS—KEY			
	Grocery store	GS	
	Restaurant	R	
	Post Office	PO	
	Bank	B	
	Leisure location	L	
	Vocational location	V	

C3—Activities and Worksheets—Real World Reading and Math

These units are used to enhance the basic reading skills of students with extensive support needs. By doing the activities, students realize the purpose of reading and calculating and gain independence in everyday tasks.

Reading Units

1. Reading a Lunch Menu
2. Reading a Newspaper
3. Reading Schedules
4. Reading Charts
5. Reading a Recipe
6. Reading a Shopping Card
7. Reading Coupons
8. Reading a Restaurant Menu

Math Units

1. Calculating the Total Cost of Groceries
2. Calculating a Restaurant Bill

Lesson: Restaurant Menu

Objectives:
1. The student will read a menu and choose two items.
2. The student will calculate the cost of their meal, including tax and tip.

Materials:
1. Menu
2. Cue Cards
3. Calculator
4. Pencil and scratch pad

Weekly—Practice reading menus for fast food and table service.
Monthly—Introduce a new menu.

Procedure:
1. Teacher—Explain the different categories of the menu and contents of each.
2. Student—Repeat the category and give examples of each.
3. Student—Read the items under each category, with assistance as needed.
4. Teacher—Discuss the items in a healthy meal, using one item from each category.
5. Student—Choose one item from each category. Write it on the pad with the price.
6. Student—Add up the total of the items chosen.
7. Teacher—Review information from prior lessons about calculating tax.
8. Student—Calculate tax and add it to their total.
9. Teacher—Review information from prior lessons about calculating tip.
10. Student—Calculate tip
11. Teacher—Tell each student that they have a specified amount of money.
12. Student—Subtract the total from the amount, and the tip from the remainder.

Evaluation—Small groups with teacher or assistant
1. Each student reads their menu choice.
2. Each student describes the calculation details.

Teacher—Record accurate data. Make instructional decisions based upon students' accuracy.

DINNER MENU

HAMBURGER PLATTER
Beef patty on toasted bun $4.95
with tomato, lettuce, onion
French fries and salad
with cheese $5.50

SANDWICHES

All served with french fries or salad

CHICKEN CLUB $3.60
Sliced Chicken, lettuce, tomato,
swiss cheese, and bacon

HOT ROAST BEEF $2.99

HOT TURKEY $2.50

HAM AND CHEESE $1.99

GRILLED CHEESE $1.50

BEVERAGES

Milk $0.75
Juice $1.00

Iced Tea $1.25

Hot Tea $1.00

Coffee $1.00

Soft drinks

Large $1.50

Small $1.00

Milkshake $2.50

SALADS

CHEF SALAD $3.99
Ham, turkey, cheese,
tomatoes and hard
boiled egg slices on
crisp greens

FRUIT SALAD $4.50
Fresh fruit in season

DINNERS

COUNTRY FRIED CHICKEN $6.99
Includes a salad, rolls, and baked
potato

SPAGHETTI $4.99

ROAST BEEF $5.50
Served with a salad, vegetable
and baked potato

STEAK $7.99
Served with a caesar salad
and baked potato

DESSERTS

Fresh Fruit $2.00

Pie $2.50

Ice Cream $1.50

Cake $2.99

DINNER MENU
Calculator Practice—Week 1

NAME: _____ DATE: _____

DIRECTIONS:

   1. **Use a local restaurant menu**
   2. **Add up the total cost of the bill**
   3. **Figure out tip**
   4. **Add in tip to get total cost of the meal**

DINNER MENU	
Hamburger Platter	$
Shake	$
Pie	$
Total	$
+ Tip	
= Total Cost of Meal	

ASSESSMENT	SCORE	%
1. Located Items Correctly	/10	
2. Correct Prices	/10	
3. Calculator (added correctly)	/5	
4. Figured Tip Correctly	/5	

Activity: Reading a Shopping Card
Objective:

1. The student will learn how to read a shopping card in order to locate the correct item by brand, size, and type.
2. The student will figure out how much the total of the items will cost.

Procedure:

From a collection of items and a set of shopping cards, students match the items:

1. Select up to four cards.
2. Locate the item.
3. Write the price on the card.
4. Calculate the total prices on all cards.

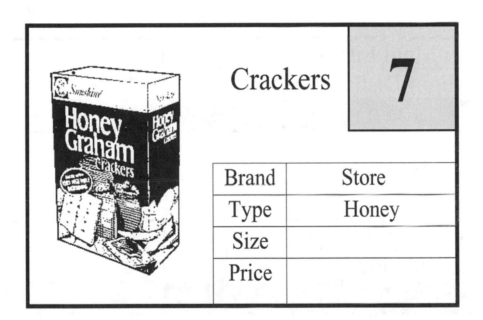

Crackers	7

Brand	Store
Type	Honey
Size	
Price	

	7

Crackers

Brand	Store
Type	Honey
Size	
Price	

CALCULATOR PRACTICE

Name: _____ **Date:** _____

Directions: Add each of the shopping lists:
- a. Locate the item and price.
- b. Write them in the column next to the item.
- c. Go to the next item and repeat until the list is finished.
- d. Write in the total you get.

1. Penn Maid Lite Sour Cream	$
Sunlight Dish Soap	+ $

2. 14 oz. Minute Rice	$
Shur Fine Frosted Flakes	+ $

3. Weis 2% Milk–1/2 gallon	$
ERA Plus Laundry Detergent	+ $

C4—Sample Behavior Program—Classroom Behavior Program

Class Rules

1. Follow directions.
2. Act appropriately and respectfully.
3. Use proper communication.

Rewards

Used to encourage and reinforce appropriate behavior.

Social Rewards—See sample awards
Praise
Encouragement
Nonverbal acknowledgment—thumbs up
Five minutes free time
Five minutes to interact with a peer

Points - "money" connected to Banking Unit

For three periods a day, students may receive up to four points an hour for positive behavior. Money accumulates for one week. 4 points = $.25

Consequences

First Reminder	Free
Second Reminder	Lose 1 point from point chart
Third Reminder	Lose 2 points and 5 minutes of free time
Fourth Reminder	Lose 3 points and 10 minutes of free time and e-mail to parents

Fines - $.25

Not prepared with pencil and paper
Materials not put away
Lost locker key
Lost other items

POINT CHART

KEY FOR POINTS: 5 - EXCELLENT 4- EXCELLENT W/ONE WARNING 3 - GOOD 2 - FAIR 1 - POOR 0 - EXTREMELY POOR										
TIME	MON	RULE	TUES	RULE	WED	RULE	THURS	RULE	FRI	RULE
8-11										
11-12:30										
12:30-2:30										
TOTAL	/		/		/		/		/	

TOTAL POINTS FOR THE WEEK:_____/_____

WEEKLY AWARDS

GREAT WORK Awards are given out throughout the week when a student has done the best work on an assignment or in a group. These certificates are worth one voucher that is saved to buy free things at our convenience mart open in the afternoons.

Two **INCENTIVE CHECKS** are given out each afternoon—one for the most improved and one for excellent behavior shown that day. These checks are worth $2.00 and put into students' savings/checking accounts.

At the end of each week, the students can possibly earn either a **WOW award or an IMPROVEMENT Award**.

WOW Awards are given to students who do not lose any points all week on their behavior charts.

IMPROVEMENT Awards are given out to the students who improve their scores from last week.

Both of these awards are big deals.

MONTHLY AWARDS

At the end of the month, students can receive several other awards:

V.I.P. Award: Shows the most improved progress in an area on which the class is working that month.

TOP STUDENT OF THE MONTH: This award goes to students who have not lost one point all month on their behavior charts.

IMPROVED STUDENT OF THE MONTH: This award would be given to any students who brought their overall monthly point chart scores up from the previous month.

TOP STUDENT OF THE QUARTER: This award would be given out to the student(s) who have not lost any points the entire quarter. The student would also receive a restaurant gift certificate.

MOST IMPROVED STUDENT OF THE QUARTER: This would be given out to the student who brought up his/her point score this quarter and lost the least amount of points. This student would also receive a restaurant gift certificate.

CLASSROOM AWARD

As an incentive to the whole class, an incentive chart, based on where the class is going to get a treat when downtown, can be prepared. Each week if the students get a set amount of WOW and Improvement awards, a part of the incentive chart goes up until it is completed (i.e., ice cream scoop).

The trip may be for pizza, soda, or ice cream. It is the choice of the students.

As an added incentive, every week a student gets an award, he or she gets a penny sticker on a ticket towards an "extra" like a topping or larger size soda on the teacher. This is only redeemable if the ticket is filled up by the time the trip is scheduled

C5—Classroom Banking System

The classroom behavior system can transfer into practice with a savings account.

1. Students earn money for positive behaviors—such as answering questions, helping, special rewards—and a simulated paycheck for classroom or schoolwide jobs.

2. Students may deposit money at the end of each day by getting a simulated deposit slip, filling in the amount, and adding it to their statement book, or on the computer if possible.

3. Students may withdraw "money" once a week, to purchase snacks, stamps, or leisure activities.

APPLICATION FOR OPENING AN ACCOUNT
ANYTIME SCHOOL
YOURTOWN, USA

Date of Application: _____

1. Full Name: _____
                  Last   First   Middle

2. Present Address: _____
                        Street

_____
  City   State   Zip code

3. Telephone Number: (_____) _____

4. Age: _____ 5. Date of Birth: _____

5. Sex: (Circle one) Male   Female

6. Color of Eyes: _____

7. Color of Hair: _____

8. Social Security Number: _____

PLEASE DO NOT WRITE BELOW THIS LINE

I understand the terms of the bank and will follow the rules. I will be responsible for fines I receive.

_____
                 Signature

_____
   Signature of Attending Bank Officer

_____
          Account Number

Anytown Bank

DEPOSIT SLIP

Date_____

Name:_____

Account Number: _____

CASH	
CHECKS	
Total Deposit	

Anytown Bank

WITHDRAWAL SLIP

Date_____

Name:_____

Account Number: _____

AMOUNT OF WITHDRAWAL
$

Signature:_____

ANYTOWN PAYROLL

Date_____

Pay to the Order of _____ $_____

_____

Anytown Bank
Yourtown, USA

For: **Class/Schoolwide Jobs**

_____

Payroll Manager Signature

C5—Classroom Banking System (continued)

Classroom Budget System

For students with extensive or pervasive support needs:

1. Use a picture budget.
2. Select an item to work toward.
3. Work with a budget envelope.
4. Place money in the envelope after it is earned.
5. Use the money, when it has reached the necessary amount, to purchase an item or save for another item.

MONTHLY BUDGET

WEEK 1	$1 Stamps + Letter Supplies	$3 Movies	$3 Goodie Shop	Total for the week $7

C6—Sample Lesson Plans

Subject	Money: Budget
Objectives	The student will demonstrate basic budget concepts.

Procedures	1. Once a day put money in their **budget** to use on different expenditures throughout the week and month
	
	Group 1: Will do the budget independently
	
	   a. Get out what is needed to work on budget
	   b. Follow a written list of to-do's in order to complete budget each week with minimal verbal direction
	   c. Count out what money is needed for the budget
	   d. Get out needed budget envelopes
	   e. Count money and put in budget envelopes
	   f. Put envelopes away when finished
	   g. Put budget notebook away when finished
	
	Group 2: Will do the budget with support
	
	2. When **activities arise that use money from budget**, student gets out envelope and put money in wallet
	
	IEP Short-term goals for this activity:
	
	1. To follow a simple budget
	2. Carry out task to completion independently with little assistance
	3. Stay organized by having only what is needed to do a task
	4. Get needed materials for different areas and be prepared to work

Text/Materials	Budget, budget envelopes, money, wallet, budget notebook
Evaluation	The accuracy of the budget

C6—Sample Lesson Plans (continued)

Subject	Money: Banking
Objectives	Complete simulated bank transactions and forms needed

Procedures	Banking
	
	1. At the end of the day students in **Group 1** will work on **banking skills:**
	   a. Get out needed materials
	   b. Count money earned that day for points they earned on their behavior sheet and write it on their deposit slip
	   c. Count quarters they earned throughout the day and write the amount on their deposit slip
	   d. Deposit any behavior checks or paychecks earned that week
	   e. Add up total deposit and write it in their transaction book
	   f. Add deposit to balance to get a new total balance for the day
	   g. Put everything in bank bag and deposit it in the bank box
	   h. Students are responsible for putting everything away
	
	2. At the end of the day students in **Group 2** will work on **banking skills:**
	   i. Get needed materials
	   j. Count money
	   k. Write their full name where needed on slip or back of check
	   l. Deposit the money in the box
	   m. Put everything away
	IEP short-term objectives: (Group 1)
	   a. Fill in the correct information in the different areas on the deposit slip
	   b. Count the cash amount
	   c. Count the cash and check amount using a calculator to get the total deposit
	   d. Write the money amount in the correct account area
	   e. Make a withdrawal
	   f. Fill in the transaction in book
	   g. Carry out task to completion independently with little assistance from an adult
	   h. Stay organized by having out only what is needed to do a task without reminders
	   i. Remember to get out needed materials for different areas and be prepared to work
	IEP Short-term objectives: (Group 2)
	   a. Fill in the correct information in the different areas he or she is capable of doing on the deposit slip with assistance
	   b. Count the cash amount
	   c. To remember to get out needed materials for different areas and be prepared to work
	   d. Stay organized by having out only what is needed to do a task without reminders

Text/Materials	Budget notebook, deposit slip, pencil, calculator and any money/quarters earned earlier that day, bank book, bank bag, quarter counter
Evaluation	Groups 1 & 2—Check and record accuracy completing form, counting cash

C7—Letter Writing

ACTIVITY: WRITING LETTERS
OBJECTIVE: The students will write a letter using a guided format.
Letter#1: Rough Draft of Parent Letter

Rough Draft of Parent Letter

Date:_____

Dear Mom and Dad,

Hi! How are you? I am having a _____ week.

This week in school

My favorite subjects have been:

_____

_____

_____

My favorite activity this week was:

_____

_____

_____

Special events that we are doing this week are:

_____

_____

_____

Hope you had a great day!! I will write again next week.

Love,_____

C7—Letter Writing (continued)

Letter #2: Students needing support verbally, will dictate a letter.

Date:_____

Dear_____

Hi! How are you? I am having a _____ week.

This week in school

My favorite subjects have been:

My favorite activity this week was:

Special events we are doing this week are:

Hope you had a great day!! I will write again next week.

Love,_____

C7—Letter Writing (continued)

Letter #3: Using Picture Symbols

Date:_____

Dear Mom and Dad,

Hi! How are You? I am having a [thumbs up] [pointing] [thumbs down] week in school
This week in school:
My favorite subjects have been:

MONEY   BANKING   TIME TELLING   TIME CONCEPTS   PRINTING   READING   SHOPPING

My favorite activities have been:

LIBRARY   SHOPPING TRIP   COOKING   Phys. Ed.   GOODIE SHOP   JOBS

Special Events we are doing/have done this week are:

SPECIAL EVENT

WARWICK
RESTAURANT   **SWIMMING**   GAME DAY

ICE CREAM   PIZZA OR SODA   FUN WITH MUSIC
AT   AT   CLASS
CINDY'S   ROMA

So as you can see, it has been another busy week at school. I hope you are having a good day. I will write again next week. Please write when you can.

Love, _____

Appendix D—Forms

D1—The Transition from Classroom to Community

The Last Day to Practice a Skill in the Classroom

Skill_____

1. Student—Do a last practice trial of the skill.

2. Teacher—Ask students to explain what was done.

3. Student—State sequential steps in the skill.

4. Teacher—Ask students to describe what they think will be different in the community or tell students what will occur in the location:

   a. A much larger space.

   b. Many people using the location.

   c. Many, many products.

   d. And so forth.

5. Student—Repeat the anticipated new situation as closely as possible.

The First Day Doing a Skill in the Community

Skill_____

1. Teacher—Review yesterday's discussion of "In the Community"

2. Student—Repeat the process described

3. Teacher—Repeat safety rules

4. Student—Repeat safety rules

5. Move to the "Before Going" section of each location plan

D2—Task Analysis Particular to Specific Community Sites

Grocery Shopping Targets
Before Going:
1. Make a shopping list or gather the correct picture/written cards needed for the trip
2. Check for coupons (if using)
3. Make sure to have enough money for what you need
4. Check schedule/calendar for day, date, and time of trip
5. Check the weather (how to dress for the outside)
6. Check appearance (hygiene and grooming)
7. Make sure to have everything you need—wallet, money, coupons, tissues, list/cards
At the Store:
1. Get a cart/basket
2. Know which door to use
3. Get shopping list, written cards, or picture cards of what is needed
4. Get calculator
5. Get coupons (if using them)
6. Locate correct aisles by locating item needed on aisle signs or by matching the aisle # on the card to the sign
7. Locate correct department by remembering where item is located or matching the name on the card to the dept.
8. Locate item
9. Locate brand name
10. Locate type of item
11. Locate size of item
12. Locate price of item
13. Keep running total of purchases
14. Locate open checkout lane
15. Put items on counter carefully
16. Present coupons to cashier
17. Pay for groceries
a. count out the money needed to pay for the groceries
b. wait for change
c. move to the side and put change away immediately
18. Gather the bags of groceries carefully and leave the store
After Leaving the Grocery Store:
1. Load groceries into car carefully
2. Carry groceries into the house carefully
3. Unpack and put away groceries in the correct spot

D2—Task Analysis Particular to Specific Community Sites (continued)

Restaurant Achievement Targets
Before Going:
1. Decide where you are going
2. Decide how much you are going to spend
3. Check schedule/calendar for day, date, and time of trip
4. Check the weather (how to dress)
5. Check appearance (hygiene and grooming)
6. Make sure to take materials needed—wallet, money, tip guide, comb, and tissues
At a Fastfood Restaurant:
1. Know which door to go in
2. Go up to a counter or get in line
3. Decide what you would like to eat and drink before getting up to the counter
4. Tell the cashier your order
5. Tell the cashier if it is for "here" or "to go"
6. Pay the cashier
7. Wait patiently for your meal
8. Get condiments/drink before sitting down
9. Find an empty table
10. Put belongings in the proper place
11. Practice good manners while eating
12. When finished, throw papers and cup away
13. Put tray on top of the trash can
14. Gather up belongings before leaving the restaurant
At a Table Service Restaurant:
1. Know which door to go in
2. Wait for a host/hostess to seat you
3. Put your belongings in the proper place
4. Decide what you would like to order from the menu
5. Give the waiter/waitress your drink order
6. Give the waiter/waitress your food order
7. Wait patiently for the food
8. When the food/drink comes, practice good manners while eating/drinking
9. When finished, wait for waiter/waitress to clear off your spot
10. If you have time/money, order dessert
11. Wait patiently for the check
12. Decide how much tip you are going to give the waiter/waitress using a tip guide, leave tip on the table
13. Pay for your meal through the waiter/waitress or up at the cashier
a. hand the check to the cashier
b. count out the money needed to pay the check
c. wait for change
d. move to the side and put change away immediately
14. Gather your belongings before leaving the restaurant

D2—Task Analysis Particular to Specific Community Sites
(continued)

Post Office Achievement Targets
Before Going:
1. Check schedule/calendar for day, date, and time of trip
2. Check the weather (how to dress)
3. Check appearance (hygiene and grooming)
4. Gather necessary materials—wallet, money, tissues, card/letter(s)
At the Post Office:
1. Know which door to use
2. Wait in line for the next available clerk
3. Ask for what you need (stamp)
4. Pay for your stamp
a. count the money needed to pay for the stamp
b. wait for change
c. move to the side and put change away immediately
5. Move to the next counter and place stamp on the envelope in the correct spot
6. Mail the card/letter in the correct slot by looking at the city in the mailing address
7. Make sure to have all belongings before leaving the post office

Leisure Activity Achievement Targets
Before Going:
1. Check schedule/calendar for day, date, and time of trip
2. Check the weather (how to dress)
3. Check appearance (hygiene and grooming)
4. Gather up necessary materials to take on the trip
Skills Used at a Leisure Activity:
1. Buying a ticket/paying fee for activity
2. Acting appropriately while at the activity
3. Practicing good hygiene and grooming while at the center (after swimming)
4. Buying a drink or snack while at activity

GROCERY SHOP

	**BELT PACK**
 16 SOUR CREAM	**SHOPPING CARDS**
	**MONEY**
	**WALLET**

D4—Problem Solving Areas

Area	Problem-Solving
Grocery store	Can't find an item, out of that item or don't sell it anymore, long lines, in a hurry
Restaurant	Don't have the brand of soda you like, don't like something on your plate, don't want ice in soda or a topping that is included with a sandwich
Post Office	Which slot do I mail the card/letter in?
Movie	Movie is sold out, time of move, not enough seats for the group to sit together
Public bus	How much change do I need? What if I don't have the exact change? What if there are no seats?
All areas	What do I need to take with me? What day and time can I go? What do I need to wear?

Pedestrian Safety Achievement Targets
Before Going:
1. Check the weather (how to dress), gather materials
Skills needed when out walking:
1. Stop at the corner/by the car
2. Look all ways before crossing the street or parking lot
3. Cross quickly
4. If at a signal, wait for the "WALK" or green light before crossing
5. Cross in the crosswalk
6. Watch for turning cars while crossing
7. Always stay on one side of the sidewalk
8. Never block an entrance/exit of a public place
9. Act appropriately while walking

Public Bus Achievement Targets
Before Going:
1. Check schedule/calendar for day, date, and time of trip
2. Check the weather (how to dress)
3. Check appearance (hygiene and grooming)
4. Check the bus schedule for bus stop, bus number, and what time the bus arrives
5. Gather up necessary materials—wallet, money, tissues, bus schedule/info
On the trip:
1. Get to the bus stop a little early
2. Wait patiently for the bus to arrive
3. Have money ready
4. Pay
5. Find an empty seat
6. Act appropriately while riding the bus
7. Watch for bus stop to get off
8. Push strip to let the driver know that you want to get off
9. Get off bus quickly

Appendix E—Forms

E1—Checklists

A Portion of a Teacher-Made Student/Parent Checklist Designed for Transition Planning

1. What kind of job do you expect to do when you finish school?
2. Do you need special training to do the job of your choice?
3. Do you want a part-time job in the area of your interest?
4. What kind of living arrangement do you see yourself in when you are 25 years old?
5. How much help do you need to be ready to live in the type of housing you have listed as your first choice?
6. What kind of family support do you expect to have when you are 25 years old?
7. How will you manage your money?

A Few Key Questions To Ask a Store Manager Prior To Conducting Instruction in That Location

Location_____

Manager_____

Product or Service _____

1. What do you expect your patrons to be able to do in your location?

2. What type of academic skills do patrons need in your location?

3. What type of help is your staff able to provide to your patrons?

4. What type of behavioral expectations do you have of your patrons?

E1—Checklists

A Possible Portion of a Planning Teacher Checklist

Student _____ Date _____

1. What are the interests and preferences stated by the student and family?

   a. Employment_____

   b. Training _____

   c. Living _____

   d. Leisure _____

2. What level of instruction does the student need to be independent in the desired areas?

   a. Employment_____

   b. Training _____

   c. Living _____

   d. Leisure _____

3. How will we sequence the skills needed throughout the remainder of this student's school years?

   _____

   _____

   _____

4. What portion of this plan needs specialized instruction?

   _____

   _____

   _____

E2—Assessment Data Sheets

Example of Checklist

Job Skills Checklist—Classroom Jobs

Evaluator: _____   Month: _____

Quarter: 1 2 3 4

Directions: Evaluator will place a checkmark in the correct column based on the Key

Key: 4 = Independent 3 = Verbal Reminders 2 = Physical Reminders 1 = Total Assistance

Jobs	Clean Tables Susie				Blackboards Bill				Mail & Delivery John				Teacher Asst. Bobby				Office Helper Christine			
Benchmarks / Rubric #'s (Students)	4	3	2	1	4	3	2	1	4	3	2	1	4	3	2	1	4	3	2	1
1. Directions																				
a. Follows routine																				
b. Follows verbal directions																				
c. Gets out needed materials																				
d. Listens, indicates by repeating																				
e. Completes task with minimal assistance																				
f. Completes a task in a required amount of time																				
g. Stays on task																				
2. Proper Manners																				
a. Makes acceptable comments																				
b. Displays acceptable behaviors																				
3. Communication Skills																				
a. Uses appropriate volume																				
b. Expresses needs appropriately																				
c. Acknowledges others																				
d. Uses mood manners																				
e. Expresses emotions appropriately																				
Health: Safety Issues																				
a. Maintains general safety (water, spills)																				

Time Concepts Group 1

Month: _____   Quarter: _____

Students					
Calendar					
Read written material					
Identify words: calendar events					
Read a weekly calendar and locating information needed to answer questions					
Read a monthly calendar and locating information needed to answer questions					
Schedule					
Read written material					
Identify words: events					
Follow a daily to-do list by identifying what needs to be accomplished					
Locate today's schedule					
Locate schedule events needed to answer questions					
Time concepts (daily time concept review)					
Apply day concepts in everyday life concepts being worked on:					
Apply month concepts in everyday life concepts being worked on:					
Apply week concepts in everyday life concepts being worked on:					

E2—Assessment Data Sheets (continued)

Shopping Assessment Progress Sheets: Group____   Quarter: 1 2 3 4

4- Independently 2- Physical assistance 3- Verbal assistance 1- Total assistance					
Students					
Health					
Adjusts clothes properly					
Wears the proper clothing for the weather					
Washes hands					
Cleans face					
Keeps hair neat and combed					
Social Skills					
Makes a hygiene/grooming check					
Takes: shopping cards					
money					
wallet					
coat, gloves, and hat					
umbrella					
tissues					
pencil					
purse/waist pouch					
Reading: Pictures					
Identifies what he or she is buying					
Math: Number Recognition					
Locates aisle # by matching to the shopping card					
Locates aisle # thru verbal directions					
Locates price					
Reading: Written Word					
Locates item on aisle sign					
Locates category of item on sign					
Identifies item					
Identifies brand					
Identifies type					
Identifies size					
Locates item by brand					
Identifies type					
Identifies size					
Reading: Pictures					
Matches picture to item					
Locates item through verbal directions					

Math: Calculator					
Calculates total of purchases being made by adding up the prices					
Health					
Car/van—wears a seatbelt					
Pedestrian—looks all ways before crossing parking lot					
Store—uses a shopping cart safely					
Keeps personal items in a safe place					
Social Skills While Shopping					
Follows verbal directions—locates items					
Listens—indicates by repeating					
Stays on task					
Uses appropriate language					
Uses appropriate behavior					
Displays courtesy towards others					
Moves when someone needs to be in that area (community)					
Handles only items buying					
Maintains an appropriate voice volume					
Acknowledges others					
Social Skills When Making the Purchase					
Locates open checkout (verbal directions)					
Has wallet ready when paying (gets out needed materials)					
Remembers to wait for the change (routine)					
Remembers to wait for the receipt (routine)					
Remembers to put change/receipt away (routine)					
Math Skills: Number Recognition					
Reads the dollar amount needed					
Reads total amount needed					
Math: Counting					
Counts out what is needed using 1. $1 bills					
2. multiple bills					
3. bills & coins					
Estimates: will add "one more" to make up the coin part of the total					
Estimates: will "dollar up" when counting out money needed					
Health					
Remembers to put wallet back in safe place					

E2—Assessment Data Sheets (continued)

Sight Words—Safety Words										
IEP Goal: When presented with a word, the student will verbally identify the word with 100% accuracy										
Key: + = correct, – = incorrect										
Students:	Stop	Exit	Men	Women	In	Out	Danger	Poison	Caution	Walk

E3—Sample Rubric For Social Behavior

IEP Objective:	The student will say please, thank you, and no thank you when ordering food at a restaurant.			
Rating	**4**	**3**	**2**	**1**
	Always uses please, thank you, and no thank you.	Frequently uses please, thank you, and no thank you.	Uses please and thank you inconsistently.	Seldom uses please or thank you.

Students	Location	Dates								

E4—Performance Graph

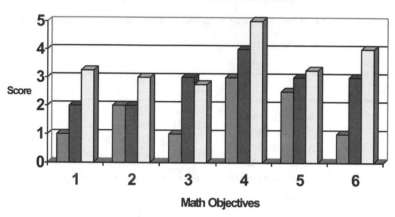

John Smith—Academic Math

4	3	2	1
Always uses please, thank you, and no thank you.	Frequently uses please, thank you, and no thank you.	Uses please and thank you inconsistently.	Seldom uses please or thank you.

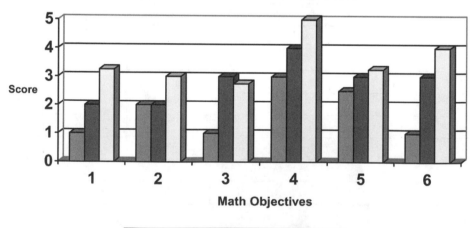

John Smith—Academic Math Goals

4	3	2	1
Mastered >85%	Satisfactory 70%-85%	Unsatisfactory 60%-69%	No Progress <59%

Appendix F—Forms

F1—Maintenance Schedules

Slow Acquisition/ Maintenance

Acquisition Time: Daily, two weeks, with verbal prompts throughout the task

Maintenance Schedule:
       Daily, for one week, with a verbal prompt at the onset of the task
       Daily, for one week, with a verbal prompt the first day, then as needed
       Daily, for one week, with prompts only when requested
       Three times a week, for two weeks, with prompts only when requested
       Three times a week, for two weeks, with no prompts
       One time a week, for two weeks, with no prompts
       One time biweekly, for a month, with no prompts
       One time a month, with no prompts, for four months

Rapid Acquisition/ Maintenance

Acquisition time: One day with minimal prompts

Maintenance Schedule:
Once a week, for one month, with no prompts,
or, written prompts as needed
Once a month for three months
Only as needed
Use the student to demonstrate the skill or
to provide a peer support to students who
have not mastered the skill

F2—Generalization Schedules

Generalization Schedule—Skill Approach

Skill	Location
Time management	Preparing for work Bus schedules School activities Recreational activities
Organizing belongings	School desk School or gym locker Desk or workspace at home Closet or dresser at home

Generalization Schedule—Location Approach

Location	Skills
Grocery store	Reading aisle markers Checking sizes and prices Asking for assistance Handling money
Drug store	Reading aisle markers Checking sizes and prices Asking for assistance Handling money
Department store	Reading aisle markers Checking sizes and prices Asking for assistance Handling money

Classroom Generalization Schedule

Skill	Initial Instruction	Implementation	Instructor	Materials	Perf. Level
Laundry	School	Laundromat on Third Ave.	Mrs. Erb	G.E.	
Generalization:	Community Locations (3)		Assistant (2)	Materials (3)	
Laundry	home		mother	Maytag	
	Clean World on Market St.		Mrs. Smith	Speed Queen	
	Wash and Dry on Main Blvd.		Mrs. Smith	Whirlpool	

(Performance Level I=independent   W=written prompts   V=verbal Prompts
P=physical prompts)

F3—Communication Devices

Communication—Newsletter Clip

Community-Based Instruction

This month's community plans include using public recreation areas. Early in the month, we will visit the local sports complex. Our instructional tasks will include scheduling times in the game room, checking the pool hours, and having refreshments at the snack bar. Later in the month, we will make several visits to the town park. We will emphasize rules and regulations, appropriate use of the equipment, and plan a picnic.

How can you help? If these are areas that your family frequents, please draw attention to those items we are emphasizing in the school program. If you do not frequently visit these recreational areas, would you consider an outing to the park? Your home participation will provide added practice [maintenance] and a chance to experience these locations with relatives [generalization]. It will also be fun!

Communication—Questionnaire

Community-Based Instruction—Using the Public Library
What activities do you feel are most important when using the public library?

_____

The format for using the library parallels other community locations.

We will emphasize: Safety issues, appropriate behavior, services available, methods to access information, getting assistance, proper use of the facility, layout, and using the service provided.
What items would you like your young adult to learn at this facility?

_____

What particular area of this location would you like him or her to experience?

_____

If we were to use, borrow, or buy an item from the library, what would it be?

_____

F3—Communication Devices (continued)

Communication—Chart

Location	Areas of Instruction	Maintenance	Generalization	Home Support
McDonalds	Ordering	3 visits	Burger King	McDonalds—lunch
	Paying	6 visits	Pizza Hut	Paying—anywhere
	Checking change	3 visits	Mini-Mart	Checking change—anywhere

Communication— Memo

Just a Reminder
Who: Jason Smith
What: Going to Midtown H.S. with the baseball team
Where: Anytown M.S. to Midtown H.S.
When: April 7, 2001
        2:00 p.m. - 6:00 p.m.
                        Teacher

Communication—Volunteers

Maintaining and Generalizing Skills
Volunteer Fact/Procedure Page

Over the course of a year, we visit many places and work on many skills. From time to time, we revisit a location or try a familiar skill in a new location. These concepts are known as Maintenance or Generalization Activities and are aimed at helping students maximize skills.

Communication—Volunteers

Dear Mrs. Miller,

    Our program works because you have devoted every Tuesday all year to accompany students on CBI. Thank you! Our students learn valuable skills because of your support.

                        Principal